SILVER LINING

The Story of
SUMMER, SNOW, *and* SKY

L.A.FIELD

WESTBOW
PRESS®
A DIVISION OF THOMAS NELSON
& ZONDERVAN

WestBow Press books may be ordered through booksellers or by contacting:

WestBow Press
A Division of Thomas Nelson & Zondervan
1663 Liberty Drive
Bloomington, IN 47403
www.westbowpress.com
844-714-3454

ISBN: 978-1-6642-2174-1 (sc)
ISBN: 978-1-6642-2175-8 (hc)
ISBN: 978-1-6642-2680-7 (e)

Library of Congress Control Number: 2021904622

Print information available on the last page.

WestBow Press rev. date: 06/15/2021

Contents

Acknowledgments

This is not only my story; it is our story—my husband's, our sons', and mine. I would like to thank Ash—my best friend, kindred soul, and champion—for standing by me through every moment of pain and for lifting my face towards what is possible with God. Thank you for not giving up, even when I did. You are a true example of tenacity, hope, and wisdom. I love the way you love God, our boys, and me.

I give thanks to my loving family and friends. Without your support, prayers, generosity, kindness, and encouragement, our story would be very different. Thank you for your constant love in our tough times. Thank you for mourning with us and for celebrating with us.

I thank the incredibly dedicated doctors, nurses, and medical staff that helped us through our challenges with fertility. We cannot thank you enough for your professionalism, care, and support during those struggles.

Thank you to our boys. You are each a special part of our lives, and we thank God every day for you! Mummy and Daddy love you now and always will!

And finally, but most importantly, thank you, Lord, for not only creating us as unique individuals and being with us in every moment of this journey but also for the sacrifice that you made two thousand years ago so that our story did not end with death. Thank you for your hope in our distress. Thank you for turning our sorrow into joy. Thank you for giving us beauty for ashes, and thank you for allowing us to live this new chapter with a renewed passion and dream for our future. I will be eternally grateful for everything you have done. I remember and will tell of your wonderful works all my days, even until my last breath.

Introduction

Lifting the tiny, fleecy sock, I search for its pair amongst the bundle of miniature clothing spread out chaotically on the dining table. Placing the mislaid sock aside, I hold up a light blue grow suit and smile to myself as I begin folding it neatly. The soft fabric gently brushes across my fingers as I place the grow suit down on the pile of clothing below. So many changes in such a short period of time have taken place in our lives over the past few years. As I steadily sort and fold the remaining clothes, the mislaid sock continues to elude me. I search right to the bottom of the laundry basket as I contemplate how blessed we are to have so many little outfits.

Under pressure to complete my chores in less than half an hour, I quickly pack away the clean laundry and scurry to the bedroom to remake our bed. Tiptoeing past the nursery, I hold my breath and tense every muscle in my body as I creep past the door without making a sound. My eyes catch a glimpse of the photos on the nursery door. My heart skips a beat to see the sweet, innocent faces on the photos strategically placed at my eye level. I dare not breathe for fear that any sound may disturb the sleep of our precious children. For over seven years, I longed for this season. As taxing as motherhood can be, I would not want to be anywhere else. The time, energy, and persistence it has taken us to live out the conviction of God's promise for our lives regarding becoming parents, coupled with the turbulent events along this passage, have been worth it. Intimate details of the trauma experienced on our way towards parenthood, carefully recorded in my journal, are the source and foundation of this tale. This is our story of loss and hope as we trekked through the valley of subfertility and grief. This is our account of how Summer, Snow, and Sky led us through stormy seasons to find our own precious silver lining.

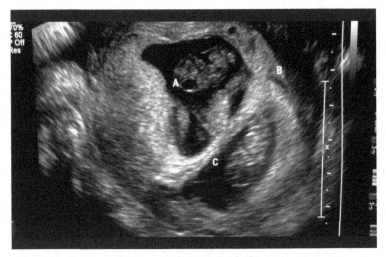

Ultrasound of triplet babies.

1

THE PROMISE OF SPRING

"Congratulations! You're pregnant with triplets!"

I was stunned into silence at the words I had just heard. It was as if someone had sent an electric current through my body. My mind was struggling to process the meaning of those words. *Triplets means three, right? Three babies, three lives, three little humans in my body.* I was going to have three children. I swallowed hard and tried to comprehend this colossal announcement but failed to regain my ability to speak. I could not even think of what to say in response.

Alerted by the surprising change to my usual gregarious personality, Ash found the prolonged silence too much. He looked down curiously at me and squeezed my hand. I don't believe he had ever experienced this length of silence from me. Awkward and unsure of what to do, I rested my head back and looked up at the speckled grey ceiling. The radiologist talked through a few details of what he could see on the ultrasound scan, but my mind escaped to a scene of me holding three babies swaddled in blankets. After remembering to breathe, I let out a huge sigh and swallowed again, smiling back up at Ash. God is able to do exceedingly and abundantly above and beyond anything I could ever ask, think, or imagine (to paraphrase Ephesians 3:20 NIV). This ran through my mind as we finished the ultrasound appointment and walked out of the clinic.

Before I go any further into our story, I must fill you in on the hours, days, weeks, months, and even years that it took us to reach this point.

Ash and I had been married for more than ten years, but the fact that we had not heard the pitter-patter of little feet in our home became a constant topic of conversation at social events. It seemed odd to many that a couple so in love and clearly comfortable around children would not have a family of their own. I often dismissed their concerns by claiming that I was too selfish or too busy to add another person into the mix. The raw truth was that I was too scared to even try to become pregnant, because my medical history meant that it would be a challenge. However, if we did become pregnant, this would mean that I would be a parent, which was an even scarier prospect.

Fear crept its way into many parts of my life and clung to everything that I allowed it to. *What was I afraid of?* I feared failing as a parent, letting my hypothetical children down, and becoming someone whom they would end up being ashamed of, or worse, resenting. What I completely overlooked was the fact that the world, including my immediate world, was filled with parents and caregivers who loved their children and showed this love through thoughtful, intentional actions and words. Those people lived fulfilled and happy lives. Unfortunately, brokenness in my own life clouded my perspective and made it easy for me to focus on what was wrong in the world and overlook what was right—to see the bad but be blinded to the good.

Ash and I discussed the possibility of becoming parents very early in our relationship. My prediction was that it would probably occur as a result of someone else's pregnancy experience, through adoption. However, after God gave us a promise that we would have our own children, we kept our minds and hearts open for future possibilities. Talking about this to anyone else was difficult for me, as I struggled with doubting whether it would really happen for us and, if it did happen, whether I would have what it took to be a good mother.

Sunday, 25 August 2013

<u>Diary Entry</u>

> I went to church this morning and thoroughly enjoyed serving on the hosting team again. I love being a part of this welcoming, caring community who share our values and give both Ash and me a sense that we belong.

Church life was a priority for Ash and me, as we were both raised in faith communities. We had always valued the hope and connection that this kind of assembly brought. Although being part of this devoted group of followers had not safeguarded us from struggling with infertility, we did have access to a higher power and believed that His help was never far away.

Our doctor suggested the process of ovulation induction, as I had been diagnosed with polycystic ovarian syndrome (PCOS). We tried to become pregnant without medical intervention for a year, but as one of the symptoms of PCOS is irregular ovulation, this process proved impossible.

We discussed doing a round of follicle stimulating hormone (FSH) injections and decided to go ahead. In my naivety, I imagined that creating a new life would be the natural result of a beautiful night of intimacy with someone I loved very much. My imagination pictured a scene of two people holding hands and walking along a beach set against a pink-and-purple sky during a breathtaking sunset. Nine months later, a beautiful baby swaddled in a fluffy blanket would arrive.

My reality was somewhat different. There was nothing natural about injecting myself with needles day after day, hoping and believing that this time it would work. *Where was the romance in that?* My conviction was that our bodies were originally created to create. They were formed and fashioned to reproduce. Sin and disease entered with one rebellious decision and left us with a less-than-perfect ability to conceive and give birth. For some, including Ash and me, there were issues that made that process a little more difficult. I have met many wonderful couples that have desired nothing more than to have a baby but were unsuccessful even with the most advanced medical assistance. I have also met people who instantly became pregnant. It is one of those mysteries of life that I, for all my thinking, contemplating, and reasoning, was unable to make sense of. Nervous that Ash and I may be one of those unfortunate couples that try but are unsuccessful, we took stock of what was ahead and knew full well that this could all be for nothing. However, we had a promise from God, and although the odds were against us, we decided to face the unknown with a spark of courage.

Monday, 26 August 2013

<u>Diary Entry</u>

> This afternoon, after enjoying a cup of tea, I relaxed into our recliner and closed my eyes. I heard God say, "Have the injections. You will conceive."

This is a voice I had heard many times before. I sat still and allowed the words to sink from my head into my heart. This voice came from someone who knows me better than anyone else. It is a voice that I love to hear. It is a voice like no other. It is the voice of the Creator, the One and Only, the Divine. Suddenly I didn't feel so alone.

Sunday, 1 September 2013

<u>Diary Entry</u>

> Spring is in the air. New things are ahead! I feel as if October is going to be a very special month. Today is Father's Day.

I always knew that Ash was going to be a wonderful father. He has always been a good provider and shown care for those close to him through his thoughtfulness, generosity, and mischievous but kind nature. I have a strong hope that Ash and I will have children of our own. I have a peace in my heart to go ahead with the appointment next week with our fertility specialist. I have started thinking of names for our child. Ash suggested that Snow Field could be a fun choice.

Ash's fun-loving nature meant that his suggestions for names weren't always serious. He loved using words that worked well with our last name, amusing himself with weird and wonderful name pairings. Some of his partially serious choices were Kane and Berry, but his favourites by far were Air Field, Force Field, and Danger Field.

Wednesday, 4 September 2013

Diary Entry

> I called Mum to wish her a happy anniversary. I know today can be a difficult time for her as she remembers Dad.

My parents got married in a time when apartheid was still active in ruining people's lives in the place where I was born—Cape Town, South Africa. I remember my parents and other relatives telling me story after story of the disgusting injustices of the times. Segregation, oppression, violence, and racial prejudice filled community mindsets as the government adopted a policy of hatred. My parents struggled in a land where the colour of their skin and the suburb they lived in determined the amount of respect, or lack thereof, they received from the authorities. Marriage was challenging enough as they attempted to forge two households, traditions, and norms into one. I cannot imagine the pressure my parents had to face as they spent their first few years building their new family.

Saturday, 8 September 2013

Diary Entry

> Struggling with fear. Overwhelmed by the possibility that our attempts to become pregnant may end in disappointment. Need to pray.

Ash and I had become quite accustomed to people's endless inquiries about plans for having our own family. Our responses ranged from "not sure" to "after we grow up." We made up our minds about family planning a few years ago and decided whom we would confide in. However, this did not come easily. I understood that becoming a parent would require some major adjustments, but many people had done it in the past and survived, so why couldn't we?

That evening, as I found the most comfortable seated position on our bed, I penned a summary of my day. *What if this attempt to start a family doesn't work?* I thought as I flicked the pen in my hand. This could all come to nothing, all this effort, all this time, all this money. Hanging over the edge of a mental cliff, facing a potential spiral of doubt, I looked down to my phone, which flashed up the notification of a message. Replacing my pen with my phone, I checked the message. It was from a friend who had sent me an encouraging thought. I started to cry as I read the words of the quote: "Never give up. Great things take time." I felt tender but hopeful while reading and rereading those words, and I smiled at the possibilities ahead.

Monday, 9 September 2013

Diary Entry

> It's been four days since I had the last of the tablets, which trigger my menstrual cycle and start the whole process of ovulation induction. I'm hoping it all goes to plan. We had a great weekend. Ash and I went over to a friend's house for dinner. This couple have had their own struggles with having children but have overcome the hurdle and have been blessed with a beautiful child. I held on to the hope that we would have the same story.

Friday, 13 September 2013

<u>Diary Entry</u>

> I have nothing to complain about. Other people are
> living in far worse conditions than I could ever imagine.

Each morning, I took time to ready my spirit for the day by expressing my gratitude for the good things in my life. Then I humbly asked for those things that I needed God to provide. I said a prayer for Ash, my family and friends and asked for my life to be used as a source of inspiration and hope to those who were in difficulty.

To me, gratitude was a rare but precious commodity. It required me to focus solely on what I had, not what I did not have. I believed that happiness was rooted in a truly grateful heart. Years ago, after watching an episode of *The Oprah Winfrey Show*, I penned five things I was grateful for. I was surprised that it did not take me long to think of five things. As I read over my scribbled list on the used envelope, I felt my mood lift as energy returned to my body. Convinced that gratitude was not only good for my mind and emotions but also good for my body, I drew an outline of my hand on the bottom of the page and wrote five new things that I was grateful for—one for each finger and one for my thumb: Ash, my extended family, my friends, my health, and my relationship with a loving, kind, and all-powerful God! I closed my diary with a full and grateful heart.

Ash and I were further into the process of beginning a family of our own. I was under the care of some amazing professionals and felt confident that whatever happened, we would be okay. It was taxing, and I would much rather have fallen pregnant without assistance. However, I had come to the realization that in every situation, life presents us with a choice. We could take the opportunity to embrace the difficulty and roll with the punches; otherwise, we could become bitter and angry about the unfairness of our predicament. It was not always easy, but this was my choice. I was sobered by the fact that I lived in an affluent country, I was rich with family and friends who loved and supported me, and I had the use of all my faculties, limbs, and senses. I had at least three meals a day (sometimes more), a house I dwelled in freely, clean running water, every daily convenience available to me, and a clean, soft pillow I rested my head on at night. My difficulties in life paled in comparison to those in the lives of others.

Springtime brought warmer weather and hope of new possibilities. After breakfast, Ash and I discussed the progress of our music project and what needed to be done in the upcoming months. I was excited about this album because I believed the songs would bring hope to many people. Later in the morning, I tidied the house and listened to some music as I worked my way through the mountain of dishes. Mornings were usually my most productive times.

I reflected on one of the biggest gifts from God—Ash. From the beginning of our relationship, Ash showed me that he cared for me and would always be ready to help encourage and calm me when I needed it most. Over life's speed bumps, he constantly reminded me that no matter what happened, all would be well. He saw through the stress, self-doubt, and impatience, and helped me to focus my thoughts on that which was most beneficial. Ash was one of the best listeners I had ever met, and even though I often chose to act out in irrational ways, he was ready to forgive me. *How did I manage to find this incredible guy?*

My mind drifted back to the first time we met. Ash and I were involved in a syndicated radio programme for youth. He was moving into his new role as programme producer, and I had accepted the role as the female presenter for the show. To be honest, my motives were not entirely innocent, and I was rather interested in getting to know another person involved in the show—Frank (not his real name!). The first planning meeting we had as a team took place at the executive producer's house. I was on my best behaviour and even took a little extra care with my appearance that evening because I knew that Frank would be there.

As we all sat down to discuss the particulars of the programme, in walked Ash. He slumped into an armchair a few seats away from me, having made no attempt to enter the room discreetly. Throughout the night, this outspoken member of the team did not hold back any thought that crossed his mind. He teased and joked when we talked about the show, and he used one-liners to get the attention of those in the room. I tried to smile away my annoyance. Many times throughout the evening, I just wanted to turn to this obnoxious latecomer and tell him to be quiet, but I thought better of it, as I didn't want to risk seeming rude or intolerant. However, after expending all my patience, I quietly prayed that God would give me the strength and patience I needed to put up with this annoying person, because I was running out of my own good will. In fact, I asked God to help me to love this guy, as I knew the Bible instructed me to love other people—even difficult people. I thought it a stretch that I would 'love him', but I would settle for tolerance if it came down to it. Unfortunately, Frank did not seem to notice me at all. I can only imagine the eye rolling, irritated expressions, and insincere smiling he saw if he looked my way at all during the evening as I attempted to conceal my annoyance at Ash.

The first recording session of the syndicated radio programme went well. I promised myself that during the second session I would try not to show my nervousness. In the fortnight between recording sessions, I practised speaking clearly and rehearsed sample scripts. The most trouble I had was when I tried to pronounce some of the band names. I had not realized that I would enjoy being part of this project and that the possibility of a relationship with Frank would be a bonus. The radio studio was an exciting place to be. The room was filled with complicated technical equipment, switches, and cords I dared not touch.

Minutes before the session started that evening, I sat in the comfortable swivel chair and practised my most serious radio face. I studied the huge, expensive-looking headphones, checking my watch several times as I ran my finger nervously over my lips with some lip gloss. I wondered when my co-host would arrive. Caught up in my thoughts, I was startled awake as I heard someone at the first studio door. I pursed my lips and sat up straight. The heavy, soundproofed door swung open, and I was surprised to see Ash. The curious look on my face must have said it all, because without a moment's break he explained that Frank was no longer going to be part of the show. I was left with the knowledge that I was not only missing my opportunity to win over the guy I had been dreaming about for months but was also going to be sharing the intimate space, time, and oxygen with Ash on a fortnightly basis.

Disappointed at the idea of having to forge ahead without any prospect of seeing my love interest, I found it difficult to concentrate on the recording of the show. Steeped in disappointment, I resisted the urge to back out of my commitment to the programme. I had grown to love the idea of being part of an initiative to spread a positive message to young people around the world.

By all accounts, things with the radio programme were going well, even though Ash found great pleasure in trying to distract me while I was recording by throwing pieces of paper at me and putting pencils in my hair. Somehow I was able to get through each session. Ash was annoyingly endearing, and I even found myself laughing at his comments, anecdotes, and pranks. Little did I know that only a few weeks later, my opinion of Ash would change forever.

That revelatory day has been permanently imprinted in my mind. It was a Saturday afternoon. The executive producer explained that our recording session would be delayed by an hour or two and suggested that I relax in the waiting room. I considered going home and returning later, but I decided to stay, as I did not have anything else planned. The serenity was sucked out of the room as I was informed that Ash would keep me company. I felt awkward and uneasy, and my faded smile greeted him as he walked casually into the room. I was caught up for a moment by his bright blue eyes, kind smile, and well-placed dimples. My awkwardness subsided, and I suddenly realized what a good-looking person he was. Those few hours in the waiting room with Ash not only changed my opinion of him; they also gave me a brilliant idea to set him up with a friend of mine. I was not interested in Ash romantically, but far be it from me to keep a good marriage from happening if it was in my power to move things in the right direction.

We chatted comfortably on the waiting room couch, and I discovered that Ash was a great listener, wise beyond his years, and a compassionate soul. His sense of humour became more endearing than irritating. We chatted openly for over an hour. The film *The Sound of Music* was playing on the television in the background, and I told him that I was named after the eldest daughter in the film. Ash told me that he was named after a character in the film *Gone with the Wind*. We found out during our conversation that although we had very different ethnic backgrounds, families, and upbringings, we agreed on the important stuff, such as values and morals, destiny, and purpose. It certainly was an eye-opener getting to know someone I did not enjoy spending time with only a few weeks earlier. Ash and I became friends that afternoon and remained that way until the night we started dating about two years later. I was thrilled that my matchmaking abilities were poor; otherwise, this romantic story would have a very different ending.

Sunday, 15 September 2013

<u>Diary Entry</u>

I love my Pa, and I miss Ma so much.

My heart sank whenever I thought of my grandmother, who passed away peacefully on the first day of winter in 2011. One memory of our time together popped into my mind as clear as day. I can still picture us sitting in the kitchen together, my arms resting on the lace tablecloth. We discussed upcoming family events and I relayed a story about Ash showing me kindness. My grandmother commented on what a good husband he was. Our conversations were always filled with words of warmth and acceptance. I felt safe in her presence. That day she looked frail but in good spirits. The last few years of health issues had taken their toll on her body and her confidence, but they had not affected her ability to show love and generosity to all of us. This was one of the last times I spoke to her.

One of the fondest childhood memories I have of my grandmother is of her looking after me as a preschooler. I was her first grandchild, and she doted on me. Each day after breakfast, we would say farewell to my uncles and aunts as they went to school; then my grandmother and I would rush back to my grandparents' bed and jump under the covers and laugh. She would reset the bed covers and begin her chores for the day while I brushed my teeth, washed my face, and prepared for my day of exploration and adventure. Safety, fun, warmth, laughter, comfort, cuddles, and kindness were my experiences with my grandmother. She loved God, her husband, her family, and other people in her community—especially children.

For years she cared for her own five children in two different continents, first in South Africa, and then in Australia. She took on the incredible task and adjusted to a new life in a new country, which would have been challenging, to say the least. Fortunately for my grandparents, they spoke English fluently and had some extended family in Australia, which made their move less lonely.

After being a homemaker for many years in South Africa, my grandmother heard the first cries of a new baby, her first grandchild—namely, me. I knew that I was spoilt, being the first grandchild on my mother's side and the first female grandchild on my father's side. Not that I remembered much, but it did bring comfort to think that I was born into a coterie of love.

My grandmother recounted many times that it broke her heart to leave my mother, my father, my brother, and me in South Africa when they migrated to Australia. Many prayers were whispered through tears as she hoped and dreamed for us to be reunited with them. Five or so years later, her longing was gratified when my parents, my brother, and I stepped onto Australian soil for the first time. It was the fulfilment of one of my grandmother's own personal miracles. She cared for my siblings and me for many years. As we grew up, we also witnessed her care for many other children through her work as a home carer. Dedicating many years to lovingly tending numerous vulnerable children in our community was part of the legacy she left with us.

My grandparents were married for nearly fifty years. It seems impossible to sum up someone's life in a few paragraphs, but I would say that she was a woman of faith, tender love, elegance, and kindness. She prayed for each member of our family every day and was always ready with a generous gesture, caring word, or warm hug. My grandfather had always been the strong and dependable patriarch. He was the one who showed wisdom in the decisions he made to protect and provide for his family in the way he knew best, while maintaining a mischievous sense of humour. Whilst working full-time and raising a family, he volunteered at his local church, maintaining buildings and gardens for others to enjoy. Now retired, my grandfather continues to be a blessing to others in need. What a perfect combination. My grandmother prompted and encouraged me to pursue my spiritual walk, to value family, and to live with kindness. My grandfather continues to teach me the importance of integrity, hard work, honesty, and loyalty. My life is thoroughly blessed because of my grandparents.

Monday, 16 September 2013

<u>Diary Entry</u>

I had a strange dream about having a baby last night.

I have always believed that I am spiritually sensitive and gifted with spiritual insight. Ever since I could remember, wild and vivid dreams had filled my sleep. My mind had also frequently been occupied with visions and images of the past, the present, and the future. Those dreams and visions usually brought peace and clarity to my life. I could not remember a time when I did not have access to them; nor would I want to think of a life without them. Some of my dreams and visions were symbolic in nature, and it usually took me a while to decipher their meaning. I discovered that the best way for me to understand them was by recording them, reading over them, and, if appropriate, sharing them with trusted friends.

Tuesday, 17 September 2013

<u>Diary Entry</u>

I feel uneasy about collecting fertility medication today.

This is a whole new area that I don't know if I can handle. The doctors explained each step of the process, and from the safety of the doctors' clinic, with Ash by my side, I felt composed. But as I sat in the car, mentally preparing myself to enter the pharmacy to pick up the medication, the reality of what we have agreed to do began to dawn on me.

Other than a fleeting desire to become a nurse at the age of nine, I tried to avoid hospitals, medical procedures, or anything to do with sickness. In my experience, hospitals were associated with memories more negative than positive. Visits to sick people in hospital desperately trying to recover from stubborn illnesses with the infrequent exuberant arrival of a new baby was what I had encountered in my past. Despite this dislike of medical institutions, I was not opposed to taking medication or enduring difficult medical procedures, which is why beginning the process of ovulation induction was more time absorbing than stressful. This practice included using needles that looked intimidating. However, I convinced myself that many women had done this and survived. Some had even repeated the process several times and lived to tell the tale. I carefully stored the medication in a purple lunch box in the fridge and found a safe place for the box of needles, disposal unit, and skin-cleaning swabs. This seemed more like homework or a project to complete than building a family. The pressure to do everything correctly was immense, and a successful outcome was not guaranteed. Sometimes the whole process was all too much and the session would end in tears. I would try to control my breathing and swallow down the tears, but overwhelmed by it all, I would cry out to God in desperation. I pleaded with Him to help me as tears trickled down my cheeks.

Tuesday, 24 September, 2013

<u>Diary Entry</u>

> I had a pretty good day yesterday, which included a blood test and ultrasound scan. My follicles are growing now. The doctor is waiting for them to be a little larger, so after one more injection of FSH, they have scheduled a blood test and scan for tomorrow.

Anxiety when having injections seemed to dissipate with the increased number of blood tests. I did not even flinch at the pain of the needle breaking my skin. Most of the time, the injections were done mid-conversation with the phlebotomist in the clinic. Sometimes I would miss the whole experience of the actual injection, as I was caught up in the exchange of dialogue.

Ultrasound scans were a different thing. I was never at ease with the scanning process, but I knew that it was necessary, and I tried to remain distracted throughout those awkward events. The vulnerability of lying half-dressed on an examination bed next to a complete stranger was one I was yet to be comfortable with.

Being greeted by the flat white sheet placed strategically on the examination table as I entered the room prepared me for the uncomfortable moments ahead. The forced politeness and the hushed conversation matched the atmosphere of the dimmed room. The lowered lights from the computer and sonographer's equipment seemed to be an attempt to make the process less uncomfortable for all involved. However, my eyes never missed seeing the intimidating scanning probes jutting out of their respective holders next to the computer. My distress eased as I realized that each of these instruments played a unique role in helping me see the life that grew within.

At times during the ultrasound sessions, I turned my thoughts to the ultrasound technician. I distracted myself with thoughts about why the technician chose this profession and considered the challenges he or she possibly faced with clients. I speculated about the technician's family and his or her life outside of those four walls. I wondered whether this was what they imagined helping people in the medical field would be like. Did they become attached or compassionate towards patients who frequented those rooms? This was an odd line of thinking, but it was a welcome distraction that got me through the many appointments and kept me in a better frame of mind.

Wednesday, 25 September 2013

As my mother and I discussed the coming weekend, I manoeuvred the car into the park along the street parallel to the hospital. Struggling to concentrate amidst the distracting noise from the busy medical specialist waiting room, I turned my attention back to the conversation with my mother. The long wait became a good time to catch up on all of her news.

My mother is the most tenacious person I have known. 'Kind', 'spirited', and 'strong' are the words that seem befitting to her character. As a young wife and mother of two living in South

Africa during the eighties, she faced the outrageous injustices of apartheid. Furthermore, she struggled through one of the most difficult events of her life as she watched her brothers, sisters, and parents move away to the other side of the world. This land was chosen, as it promised to be a place people were no longer judged by the colour of their skin or the number on their identity card, but rather by the values and morals shown through their character and individual life choices.

My parents married promptly after finding out that I was to join their duo. Their wedding ceremony took place in spring, and I arrived in the autumn of the following year. The knowledge of my existence flung my young parents into a barrage of hasty life-altering decisions. I am grateful that they decided to allow my life to continue even though my existence was unexpected. Within three years of becoming parents for the first time, my mother told my father that she was pregnant again. This time the baby was a precious little boy.

My mother's journey during that decade started with a teenage pregnancy, then marriage, followed by her becoming a mother of two children and losing her extended family to a country thousands of kilometres away. The year my brother started primary school was the year we left our relatives in South Africa and joined my mother's extended family in Australia. It would be a big transition, and we would desperately miss the gatherings, the special occasions, and the closeness of our relatives and friends in Cape Town, but the prospect of allowing their children opportunities for the future was what drove my parents to make this huge sacrifice.

I miss my father every day because he taught me how to make hard decisions. Moving from Cape Town in his thirties would be a colossal adjustment in his life. My father was the second eldest of four children born to a cabinetmaker and homemaker in the Western Cape of South Africa. He was a sensitive, artistic, generous, troubled, misunderstood, attractive, humorous person who suffered his own traumas. He often shared his many stories of regret and pain once his taste for whisky or beer had been satisfied. He wrestled with a dependence on alcohol. His distressed memories of childhood, mixed with substance abuse and low self-worth, resulted in violent behaviour towards my mother. He tried to overcome the negative effects of the substance abuse in his life, and the consequences of those effects, but even his best efforts left him wanting. Suffice to say I grew up with the damaging consequences of family violence in a dysfunctional home. However, two years before my father passed away, we saw a change in his behaviour. There was a huge shift in the way he treated us, and he even took on some volunteer work in his local community to help people find work. He emulated his much-admired father in the way that he submerged himself in loving God by serving and loving others.

During our childhood, my brother and I did our best to cope. Many awkward moments were lightened by my brother's jokes, told nervously through him chewing his fingernails. As a child, my brother was a sports enthusiast. He played football and basketball, and he enjoyed talking about the professional players in each of those sports. My brother's intelligence and humour marked his personality, and he was never without friends surrounding him wherever he went. A sensitive soul, my brother also longed for peace in our home. As children, we enjoyed going to the local shopping centre, swimming pool, and parks with our friends during school holidays and weekends. Our home, although not perfect, welcomed many of our friends for play dates and sleepovers. My parents did their best to care for us and always provided for our physical needs, but they were overwhelmed at times with the responsibilities of a growing family.

My sister was born four months before my twelfth birthday. I was excited beyond belief to know that I had a mini-me to dress up, play with, and boss around. My brother and I had a good relationship, but as gorgeous as he was as a baby, he did not look his best in a dress with accessories. My sister made her entrance into the world one sunny November day while my brother and I were at school. My grandparents drove us to the hospital straight after school so we could meet our beautiful new sibling. She had the biggest eyes I had ever seen on an infant; dark, thick hair and smooth skin. She was adorable. My sister was unlike any toddler I had ever met. She was direct with her copious words, persistent in her search for attention, and a delight to have in our home. Her lively personality brought a much-needed distraction from the tension that would sometimes build up in our home. Her jet-black hair; large, round eyes; and pink cheeks resembled the features of a doll I received as a gift before she was born, in anticipation of her arrival.

I was set to work almost immediately in helping my parents care for my sweet younger sister. As I was the eldest child in the family, my duties ranged from helping to keep up with daily needs of a newborn baby to preparing meals with my mother, as well as caring for my brother. My parents were often occupied with earning a living to support their increasing number of children. We had found our rhythm as a new family of five by the time my sister was only a few months old.

The shock and surprise that my mother was going to have another baby came around my sister's first birthday. I could not believe that our number was about to increase. We were going to be the 'Daniels family of six'. My parents decided that we would need a second car and would also move into a bigger house to accommodate our growing tribe. Eleven days before my thirteenth birthday, my adorable youngest brother was born. His head was covered with a mass of dark ringlets, endearing him to every onlooker. He was a quiet and affectionate little boy who had three older siblings to tell him what to do. Gentle and thoughtful with a keen interest in his toys, my youngest brother found a special place in all of our hearts. He was always very close to our parents, and we all doted on him.

My sister and youngest brother had a special relationship, not only because they were close in age but also because we subconsciously treated them like twins. We affectionately called them 'the kids'. Who was looking after the kids? Where were the kids going? What would the kids eat for dinner? The kids were a wonderful blessing in our lives. My parents spent a lot of time taking them on excursions, trips, and outings. Wisdom comes with experience. Although I knew my parents did not have any favourites, I believed that they were able to enjoy their relationship with the kids differently to the way they were able to with my brother and me.

Attending to our baby siblings was my first experience of looking after children. Many of my friends expressed a longing to start their own families when we were in our early twenties, but to be honest, that was never my desire. I knew the hard work that came with the cute smiles, giggles, and cuddles of a baby. I remembered the endless nappy changes, baths, many loads of dirty washing, and hours of food preparation. I recounted the multiple bribing attempts to make vegetables appear tantalizing and the clean-ups after mealtimes. I cherished my younger siblings, and still do, but spending time with them when they were babies went hand in hand with hard work. My brother and I had our set chores and kept ourselves motivated as we dreamed of the moment when we would be able to train our younger siblings to take our places in those duties.

Our family enjoyed day trips, camping, swimming, barbecues, and basically anything that involved food and the great outdoors. We also spent many hours watching our favourite family television shows after dinner. Growing up in the Daniels family had both light and shade, and it set the foundations of our own future families. I knew that I would one day want some of those fun times to be enjoyed by my partner and myself, with our children, whether they were adopted, fostered, or of our own DNA.

Thursday, 26 September 2013

<u>Diary Entry</u>

> I'm scared that this process will come to nothing. I know I will be disappointed and discouraged because of everything we have invested including our time, money, and emotional effort. I can hardly believe that only a little while ago I wasn't even thinking of becoming pregnant. I have changed so much. My heart has opened up to being a mother, and I am excited about what lies ahead.

During this part of my medical journey, I learned a lot about the human reproductive system. I wished I had paid more attention in human health classes at school. Memories flooded into my mind of the time in high school when I failed a test in health education simply because I refused to study the textbook. I remembered that I argued that the textbook pictures were too graphic for my young mind. The patient, wise teacher listened to my argument, and after I had run out of steam and words, she informed me that I would need to repeat the test the following week. With my proverbial tail between my legs, I walked out of her office and down the corridor, and I opened up the textbook on the way to my locker.

<u>Diary Entry</u>

> We have a few small follicles. Ideally the follicles need to
> be much larger for us to try to conceive. I will be having
> another scan tomorrow, after more injections.

Ash and I were reassured that all was going according to plan with my blood test and ultrasound scan. The fertility nurses and our specialist doctor were tracking our progress.

Anxiety lurked in the dark spaces of my heart during the final steps of the process. I could only assume that the nervousness I was feeling stemmed from the unknown, as I had become accustomed to the physical discomforts. Desperately, I held on to the hope that Ash and I would become parents, and I wondered what life would be like with a child. *How would my body feel? Would I get morning sickness? How would our daily routines change, if at all?* Reasonably confident that we would cope fairly well with all the changes, I reminded myself that others had gone before us many times and not regretted their decision. Searching popular baby names on my phone brought with it distraction and some relief. I hoped there would be a little person with our surname soon. I even daydreamed about how I would sign the three of our names on greeting cards in the future. An image popped into my mind of me standing next to Ash for a photo, holding our gorgeous new bundle from God. Those thoughts and visualizations cheered me up. I believed that it was possible for our pregnancy to be the result of this cycle or one in the future. In the meantime, I decided to focus on the hope I held on to.

That night I had a dream.

In the dream, I was resting on my back in a boat, which was gliding slowly along a smooth river. The gentle current was carrying the boat faster and faster. I allowed the river to carry me. As I looked up to the sky, I fought the temptation to sit up to see where I was. I allowed the boat to drift along, even though I could not see where it was taking me. I relaxed my whole body and let the boat gently carry me.

Friday, 27 September 2013

<u>Diary Entry</u>

> Today is going to be our first attempt to get pregnant. I can't pretend not to be nervous. I don't even know how to feel.

We had specific instructions with the ovulation induction process. After a number of consultations, phone calls, ultrasound scans and blood tests, we were ready to begin. Somehow the idea of discovering I was pregnant worked differently in my imagination. I thought one day I would sit Ash down after work, talk to him about buying new furniture for the nursery, and then casually hold up a positive pregnancy test. Sitting in the waiting room of a fertility clinic early in the morning was not featured in my romantic idea of starting a family. The idea that a series of blood tests, injections, and ultrasound scans were involved in perfectly timing the conception of a child amazed me. A process that was always meant to be natural and the product of an intimate encounter had been, in some ways, transformed into a clinical procedure. I was grateful for the advancements in the field of medicine, and I was fully aware that without these incredible achievements, I might not have this story to tell. Yet at times it all seemed so unemotional and such a cold and distant process.

As I sat daydreaming in the waiting room of the fertility clinic, I was abruptly stirred out of my dreamy state. Glancing to the side, I saw a mother and her child taking their seat next to me on the waiting room couch. I promptly moved to my right to give them more room. The adorable child looked up at me, and I could not help but smile down at his sparkling eyes. The little boy, eager with curiosity, scanned every item on the waiting room coffee table. His mother seemed flustered and called his name several times to distract him from touching various prohibited items. I could only assume that this treasured boy was a miracle child, as his mother was in this clinic. The boy approached me, pointing his finger at my head.

"Curls," he said repeatedly.

"Yes, curls," I confirmed, smiling back at him. I playfully lifted one of the curls from my left shoulder and smiled.

He leaned closer and pointed at my hair. The little boy stretched even closer to try to touch my hair.

"No, Gabriel!" his mother warned.

"Oh, that's okay," I said, smiling at her.

"You want to touch my curls?" I asked looking down at his round, wholesome face.

I glanced across at his mother for further permission. She smiled and nodded. Then I leaned down.

"Gently, Gabriel," she instructed.

Gabriel touched a curl and chuckled to himself.

"Curls," he said with delight.

What a sweet boy, I thought as I leaned down to pick up a picture story book from the coffee table to my right.

"Trucks," I said, pointing at the front cover of the book.

"Thank you," his mother whispered as Gabriel reached to take the book.

Admiring this beautiful child as he opened the book to discover what visual treasures lay within, I heard my name called from the consultation room to my right.

"Bye, Gabriel," I said, picking up my bag.

"Bye-bye, bye-bye," he said, looking up from his book.

We waved at each other as I walked towards the door.

Hope rose in my heart as I thought about the possibility of Ash and me having our own little darling soon.

The phlebotomist greeted me warmly as I entered the room for my blood test. We discussed the weather and our plans for the weekend. He had a strong accent, and our conversation drifted to his cultural background. As I walked out of the room, I thanked him and wished him well for his day ahead.

As I sat in my car, the emotion of the situation hit me again. I leaned forward, rested my head gently on the steering wheel and closed my eyes. Whenever I had the slightest sense of optimism about this process, it was as if all the doubts flooded in to wash away my hope. *What if this cycle did not work? What if none of the cycles worked? Would I ever have the opportunity to hold my own baby in my arms?* It was as if, in that moment, my faith was shrinking under the shadow of doubt. The overwhelming sense of helplessness hovered over me, and I froze. I tried to will it away, but that was futile. I could not do this alone. After a few minutes, I came to my senses and committed the whole process to God through a quiet prayer. Tears began to form at the corners of my eyes, and the lump in my throat began to swell as I wondered why we had to go through all of this. Ash and I, for the most part, were pretty good people. We were honest, decent people, helpful to others, and generally kind to those in our world. *Why did we have to go through all of this to become parents? What had we done to deserve this?* Those may seem like the wrong questions to ask, since there are many wonderful couples in the world that by no fault of their own have tried and failed to become pregnant. Guilt and blame were not part of this journey, but it was difficult to see why this was so hard for us. The most unpleasant parts, for me, were the invasive procedures that I had to face day after day without any guarantee of a positive outcome.

After my emotions subsided, I reminded myself to be grateful for the things that came easily into my life: the love of my parents, siblings, and extended family; friends; my faith community, having all my basic needs and most of my wants fulfilled; a good vocation, education in a country with endless possibilities, my wonderful husband, and my relationship with a benevolent, loving God. Then I wiped my tear-stained face, breathed deeply, and settled myself again. I asked for strength and a clear, steady path all the way to parenthood as I drove out of the fertility clinic car park.

We've been on this family-building journey for nearly a year, as we officially met with our specialist last October to discuss the steps we may need to take.

Blessed with a GP who has dedicated her life to helping others, Ash and I could only feel gratitude. Our family doctor had always shown compassion, attention, and genuine care for her patients, and we were grateful for her help and ceaseless support.

Our fertility specialist was also a warm and personable professional. Our meetings were difficult only because we were exposed to the many limitations, risks, and possible outcomes (favourable and otherwise) of this process of having children. The fertility nurses were caring and attentive, which gave us confidence in the whole process.

I felt extremely fortunate as I reflected on the sympathetic people who had supported us on this journey.

Wednesday, 2 October 2013

Diary Entry

> Dating Anniversary for Ash and me! Today is a significant day because Ash and I started dating on this day many moons ago! I'm so grateful that I was the one he chose to share the rest of his life with.

It felt like a lifetime ago, but I still remembered how Ash and I changed once we decided to become more than friends. My parents had always thought well of Ash, and it was clear that he was going to treat his wife like a princess, but it took us nearly two years to finally realize that we would be a great couple.

My thought process was momentarily interrupted by a brief dizzy spell. From the way I felt that evening, I concluded that I was housing the beginning symptoms of a cold or the side effects of the fertility drug. I decided to discuss those symptoms with our doctor the next time I spoke to her.

Saturday, 12 October 2013

<u>Diary Entry</u>

I'm Pregnant!

I still wasn't feeling great yesterday, so I called my GP and made an appointment. I told her about my symptoms. She asked whether I could be pregnant. I answered yes, as we had been trying. She gave me a pregnancy test. It came back positive! My GP said that I am already four weeks pregnant, according to my cycle. That means that I will be due on 17th June! We celebrated together, and I called Ash straight away. I'm thrilled and so excited! I had a blood test before I went home.

Every time I eat, I feel slightly ill. I've had stomach cramps since Monday, and my breasts hurt, but I am so happy! Thank you, Lord! Thank you! Thank you!

I am hosting a fundraising event today with some of my family and friends to raise money for Orphancare Foundation in Cape Town, South Africa. We have been involved with this group for a little while. Ash and I met with the founders last year during our trip to Cape Town and spent time in the safe homes where they help abandoned and vulnerable children. They need all the support we can give because they are doing an amazing job of rescuing these precious little lives. I haven't told anyone about our baby yet. I'm still trying to process it myself. Ash and I discussed when we would let everyone know. I'm a little apprehensive about eating breakfast this morning, but I'm feeling much better today.

The elation I felt about being pregnant dwarfed the illness I was experiencing. I was completely in awe at the idea that I was actually carrying another human being in my body. Even though we had prepared, prayed, and done what we could to become pregnant with the help of our medical support team, I was still surprised that it happened; it actually worked! Ash and I were going to be parents, and possibly grandparents, one day. We were going to welcome a beautiful baby into our hearts, our home, and our lives. How incredible! I was totally stunned by God's faithfulness.

Monday, 14 October 2013

Diary Entry

> I went into the fertility clinic today for another pregnancy blood test. God, you are awesome! I am still amazed at this incredible gift! Great is your faithfulness!

Although we were 100 per cent sure that I was pregnant, a blood test with the fertility clinic was part of the process. I received a call from them later that day to confirm that the pregnancy test was positive and that I had a very high reading for pregnancy hormones. The nurse explained that this could mean that we had conceived multiple babies. There was no guarantee and no sure way of knowing until we did an ultrasound scan later in the pregnancy, but it was something they thought we needed to be prepared for.

After the fertility nurse discussed the possibility of multiple births, a cloud of worry settled over my mind. I had just become comfortable with the idea that I was not infertile, and then celebrated the prospect of being a parent, and now facing the possibility that this pregnancy was fragile was overwhelming. Keenly aware of my emotional state due to the abundance of pregnancy hormones surging through my body, I decided to put all my fear, worry, and anxiety aside for a while.

Wednesday, 16 October 2013

<u>Diary Entry</u>

> Today is the first day that I have felt good. I went for a
> thirty-minute walk through the local park.

Anxiety revisited with a vengeance as I flipped through an early pregnancy information booklet in the afternoon. I discovered that many things could go wrong in the first few months and decided that the best thing to do was pray. Instantly the tension lifted from my shoulders and neck. Instead of brooding over all the things that could go wrong, I chose to go to the source of my inner strength and read a few verses of the book of Jeremiah, chapter 29, in the Bible. This incredible book put me at ease, and I remained in peace for the rest of the day. "'For I know the plans I have for you," declares the LORD, "plans to prosper you and not to harm you, plans to give you hope and a future. Then you will call upon me and come and pray to me, and I will listen to you. You will seek me and find me when you seek me with all your heart'" (Jeremiah 29:11–13 NIV).

Friday, 18 October 2013

<u>Diary Entry</u>

> We visited our GP after a short walk around our local
> park. This appointment was scheduled to discuss my
> prenatal care, including which hospital we would like to
> be registered with.

On the way home from the clinic, Ash and I talked about the preparations required in the lead-up to Christmas. I reluctantly went along to our friend's birthday dinner. Every attempt on my behalf to act as normal as possible at the party failed. I tried desperately to focus on the conversation in the bustling, rowdy environment. I felt queasy because of all the smells and aromas wafting towards me from the freshly cooked meals on the surrounding tables. The menu did not help, as everything I thought about eating made me feel ill. I imagined my face turning pale green—the colour of the wasabi on a plate across from mine. My ability to hide the fact that I felt unwell must have worked. The only awkward moment occurred when the other guests noticed that I did not eat the entire meal I had ordered. A comment was made about my attempts to limit my caloric intake, and thankfully my ruse worked. Our friends had just recently had their first baby. He looked peaceful resting in his baby carrier.

After the confirmation of our pregnancy, I noticed myself drawn to babies. I would not say that I was overly clucky, but I had noticed a change in my interest in them.

Monday, 18 November 2013

"Congratulations, you're pregnant with triplets!"

Ash and I drove home, still recovering from the shock of this news. All I could manage were soft grunts and strained facial expressions as Ash discussed plans for our three children, who would be making their way into our home in the near future. Once we got home, words escaped me for the next while, so I wrote in my journal.

<u>Diary Entry</u>

I am pregnant with *triplets!*

I have been pregnant for nine weeks as of last Friday. I am getting better at coping with the symptoms. I will not be working for the rest of the year, as our GP advised me to take it easy. We are sharing our news with our family and close friends. Triplets usually mean a high-risk pregnancy, but we believe that we have three healthy babies.

I am experiencing severe bloating, breast changes, tiredness, nausea, stomach cramps, emotional outbursts, and superpower smelling abilities, and I have to eat small meals of fairly plain foods, such as toast. My love for hot drinks is a distant nauseating memory, and I am suffering from short-term memory loss. My conversations are cloudy and disorganized, but it is still a while before we will publicize the news.

Ash has already bought a three-seater pram for a bargain on eBay. We have been blessed with flowers and gifts from the few people who know about our upcoming parenting adventure. We were warned that multiple-birth pregnancies have a high rate of failing. The fact that we are considered a high-risk pregnancy in the medical world makes me anxious. Ash asked me to focus on trusting God.

Wednesday, 20 November 2013

<u>Diary Entry</u>

Ash has been amazing! He has taken care of me and made life a lot easier for me. Thank you, God, for an outstanding husband and friend!

In those early days marriage was hard work, but it was definitely worth it. I was blessed to have a man who loved me, was committed to me, and only wanted the best for me. We had our ups and downs through the years, as most couples do, but because we understood that love was a decision, there was no turning back. Whatever we faced, we knew that we could work through it, as long as we remained united. Ash and I learned how to communicate with each other in a healthy and caring way. We were aware of each other's love languages and tried to show respect and patience most of the time. Of course, neither of us was perfect, but it was our intention to love each other the way God created us to.

We heard from other couples that having children could put a strain on a relationship, so we decided to keep our line of communication clear and open, our conflict accounts short, and our vehicle of forgiveness in good working order. Some statistics about marriages could be depressing, but we took courage in the fact that we were both committed to staying together. There were no flawless relationships, just many, like ours, that were 'works in progress'.

We regularly attended our appointments with our midwife at the hospital. My health seemed fine, and the babies were progressing well. Everything seemed to be falling into place, and we were ready to embrace the future.

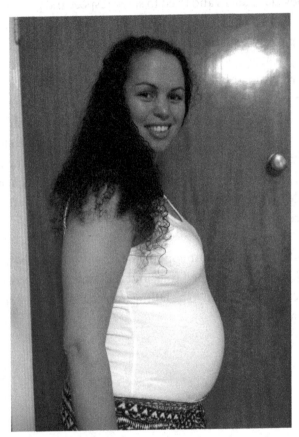

Pregnant at 20 weeks.

2

SCORCHING SUMMER DAZE

Tuesday, 3 December 2013

Diary Entry

> I will be twelve weeks pregnant this Friday. Thank you,
> God, for being so faithful. We have told the rest of the
> family about our triplets.

Ash and I let people know about the pregnancy, as my symptoms
were too hard to cover up. Their responses were priceless. Ash
recorded all of their reactions on his phone and made them into
a clip which we posted on YouTube.

Diary Entry

> Ash and I discussed my reluctance to share the news with
> everyone. I concluded that I have a fear of disappointment.
> I am scared that if I get completely caught up in this
> excitement, I will be devastated if things don't turn out
> the way I expect.

Friday, 6 December 2013

<u>Diary Entry</u>

12 weeks pregnant today! Thank you, God!

We are booked for our ultrasound. I listened to a podcast about being grateful. These are my notes from the podcast:

My antidote to complaining is to set my focus on constantly praising God and to give thanks for what He has done and will continue to do in the future. Thanking God throughout the day is helpful to my spirit, soul, and body. In refocusing my attention on others, I fight the temptation to board the self-pity train. Several times throughout the day, I ask myself, 'What am I grateful for right now?'

My mind had always been drawn towards negativity, so I needed to be intentional about staying focused on the good things in my life to remain in a positive state of mind. Regular sleep and allowing myself to be exposed to positive people, positive conversations, and positive atmospheres in my world was my most effective weapon against pessimism.

Thursday, 12 December 2013

<u>Diary Entry</u>

I had another ultrasound scan on Monday. It was very uncomfortable and lasted for forty-five minutes. We were excited to see our three babies and to hear their heartbeats. The medical staff were not able to tell the babies' genders and said they might struggle even at twenty weeks because of the babies' position in my womb. We are thankful for the love and support we have received from our family and friends.

After our baby news was announced, I received visitors, texts, Facebook messages, and calls from many people. I felt grateful for the community we were a part of. My days were relaxed and empty of activity, so I had a lot of time to think about things, ruminate, and contemplate. I was trying to be deliberately positive. Some days were better than others, as this pregnancy launched me into a vulnerable emotional state. I believed that my emotions and feelings were temporary, so although I did not ignore them, I tried not to shape my world around them.

Christmas was approaching. Ash had been wonderful in organizing all the presents and food for the numerous occasions during that busy period.

I was never a fan of Christmas. Other than enjoying Christmas pudding, this holiday was nothing more than a stressful time for me. My parents tried to make the occasion fun and exciting for us children; however, very early on I discovered that it was an excuse for alcohol to be consumed, and when this happened in our house, it was time to pay attention, as anything could happen. I remembered back to many celebrations being hampered because of the effects of alcohol. I blamed alcohol for everything that went wrong. As maturity has helped me to see, the alcohol was not evil in itself, but it was the abuse of the alcohol that could bring about devastating consequences. As a result of many disappointments, arguments, and tense moments around Christmastime, I decided when I was only a child that I would try to endure the 'festive' season but would not allow myself to be vulnerable enough to enjoy it. This kind of repressed anger and resentment that built up in me became bitterness, and internally I became the 'Grinch who loathed Christmas'. After years of living with this distorted view,

I finally took responsibility for my emotions and thoughts about the traumas of Christmases past and received healing through therapeutic conversations and prayer. I decided to change my attitude towards the whole affair. It had taken me a few years and much convincing from Ash, but I had grown to love Christmas and all that this season brought. I no longer allowed myself to wallow in negative memories; rather, I chose to make new positive ones.

Wednesday, 1 January 2014

Diary Entry

A new year! A new adventure!

We had a terrific time ringing in the New Year with friends. I spent the morning recalling all that 2013 had brought into our lives and committed the coming year to God. As I waited in my quiet place, I was led to read Jeremiah 18 in the Bible. It talked about the Potter's House. This verse stood out to me: 'The potter formed it into another pot, shaping it as seemed best to him' (Jeremiah 18:4 NIV).

I heard God whisper, 'I am preparing you.'

I am not quite sure what that meant, but owing to my swollen belly, I presumed that God was preparing me to become a mother of three children.

Tuesday, 14 January 2014

Diary Entry

As I was meditating this morning, I saw an image of Ash carrying a baby in his arms.

As the babies moved in my belly, I thought about what their little personalities were going to be. We affectionately named the triplets 'Lefty', 'Centre', and 'Righty'.

Diary Entry

I have a sense that Lefty, the baby in the left side of my belly, will be a quiet and patient person. I believe this because this baby is calm and only really moves long after the other babies do. Centre will be sociable. I believe this because as soon as one of the other babies moves, this baby starts moving. Righty will be the life of the party. This baby will be musical. I believe this because this baby is very active, and every time I sing or play music, this child moves.

Wednesday, 15 January 2013

Diary Entry

I have to go into the hospital to do a test. I am feeling more nervous than I can handle at the moment. Being at home for so long without much interaction with others has made me feel a little anxious about going out today. Also, this will not be a pleasant outing, according to what I've heard others mention about their experiences with this test. God, please help me.

The appointment was known to be arduous, but I was determined to remain positive. The clinic was crowded, and there was a mixture of unpleasant odours in the air. My nausea had improved a lot in the past few weeks, but the aromas wafting around me in that room brought those aversive sensations back, threatening me with the risk of becoming ill. The hard seat below me made it uncomfortable to sit in one position for too long. I contemplated taking a walk to the entrance of the building several times, and I longed for the comfort that the cool, fresh breeze brought as it blew in from the automatic sliding doors. As I gathered my strength to make the move, my name was called, and Ash and I made our way to the examining room.

Grateful for the padded seats in the examining room, I experienced some relief and started feeling less queasy just by walking twenty steps away from the lurking smells. After processing my details, the nurse handed me a bottle of soda. At first glance it looked like a harmless lemonade bottle, but after the first few sips, I realized that this drink was clearly medicinal. After swallowing the first few mouthfuls, I struggled against the urge to bring the drink back up. The added stress mounting in my body came from knowing that if I was unable to hold the drink in my stomach, I would have to begin the whole process from the start. Ash calmed me, for which I was thankful. However, twenty minutes in, I started to feel ill—very ill. A feeling of extreme discomfort, starting in my abdomen, rushed through my body, going all the way to my head. I could feel my cheeks burning as beads of sweat formed on my nose and forehead. Ash alerted the nurse, and I was hastened into a smaller room next to the waiting room. I reclined on the bed, and the nurse placed a cool cloth on my forehead as I quietly whispered a desperate prayer. After a few minutes, the nausea subsided and I was able to complete the glucose drink. Being out of control of my bodily responses was exhausting.

As unsettling as this experience was, it did not come close to the horrendous encounter which we were about to have.

Monday, 20 January 2014

<u>Diary Entry</u>

> As I was waiting on God, I sensed a stirring of a new thing in my heart—a vision for something He is inviting me to be a part of. It was about helping people. I thought of South Africa, and then I saw an image of a small schoolhouse.

After looking back on the drawing in my journal, I contemplated what this could mean. South Africa—Cape Town in particular—has found a special place in my heart. During past visits, Ash and I had witnessed the hardships that many decent individuals and families there endured. Several of our conversations had been immersed in ideas for helping those in need, and we had even discussed how we could practically help those God had directed us to.

Having felt tired and uncomfortable for the past few days, I allowed my thoughts to take a well-deserved break and decided to nap for the rest of the afternoon.

Sunday, 26 January 2014

<u>Diary Entry</u>

> Something doesn't feel right this morning. I have noticed a shift in my body. I called the midwife at the hospital, and she explained what I needed to look out for. I tried to

rest but felt uneasy that this was not normal. God, please
help me! You are faithful. You are good. I trust you.

As I sat in the Pregnancy Assessment Unit, I focused on the
conversations beyond the curtains. My parents-in-law had kindly
dropped me at the hospital to be assessed. The midwife at the
desk asked me a few questions and tried to calm my nerves. There
were several other patients in the room, all being attended to at
different intervals.

After having my file processed, the midwives and doctors
thoroughly examined me. I tried not to allow anxiety to creep
in. Each time I thought of what could go wrong, my hammering
heart took over. I knew this was not good for the babies, so I tried
to calm myself by thinking of a positive outcome. I prayed and
meditated on some promises from the Bible, which was helpful.

The midwives were patient and attentive. I replied to their many
requests in my raspy voice. Alone, scared, and desperate, I sat
forlorn on the cold leather chair as I waited for answers. Whispered
prayers of desperation were spoken as I sat behind the privacy
curtain in the assessment booth.

Engrossed by my thoughts, I was startled when Ash arrived.
Staring into his familiar, kind eyes, I held back the tears as I
frantically explained events up to that point. His warmth and
strength were exactly what I needed at that moment. We waited
for the medical staff to return with updates. I did not speak,
mostly because I did not have anything to say. Ash held my hand
and sat on the plastic chair next to me. As the minutes ticked past,
I sobbed quietly and pleaded with God. I begged that he would
stop whatever negative changes were happening. I sniffed back
more tears as I tried to relieve the soreness in my throat with a
few sips of water from my drink bottle.

A young doctor spoke to us briefly and invited us to another examining room. There was almost a spring in her step, and I envied her lightness of heart. The doctor appeared to have a kind and generous spirit. I waddled towards the room; Ash followed with my handbag and water bottle in hand. We were ushered into a private, dimly lit room.

The doctor instructed me to prepare for the examination and left the room. As soon as she was gone, my tears gushed out and I released the tension that had built up in my chest. Ash reassured me and tried to help me organize myself in readiness for her return. When she reappeared, she did a more invasive procedure and then discussed our situation. The doctor calmly explained the possible outcomes, and I immediately began to relax. There were no guarantees, but I felt better about this situation than before I entered the hospital.

We returned to the waiting area, and after a short while, a medical team visited us to discuss my current condition. These doctors seemed less hopeful, so my anxiety began to rise again. The doctors came to the conclusion that I could be going into preterm labour. The medical staff outlined the possible outcomes for us. I felt the fear begin leaking into all my thoughts. My only response to their report was to blurt out in a shaky voice a sentence about our faith in God. They showed great respect and continued to instruct us on the next steps in my care.

Spending the night in hospital away from Ash was certainly not what I had expected, but if resting made a difference to my condition and saved us from a preterm labour, I was willing to stay as long as I needed to. Restless sleep coupled with regular vital checks made for a disrupted night's rest. The curtains were drawn, but from what I could make out, the lady next to me had just given birth to a baby girl.

After being in hospital overnight, there was a change in my body. Desperately needing encouragement and believing in the power of agreement in prayer, I texted a few family members and close friends to let them know about our situation. My eyes flooded with tears as I was overwhelmed by their positive responses. I credited my improvement to the prayer requests that I had sent out via text message. An uncomfortable but lengthy sleep set me up for a better day. Periodically, midwives attended my bed to check my vital signs, and I tried to remain in a positive state of mind. I listened to the conversations in English and in a variety of other languages coming from the hospital beds in the room.

The next morning, the nurses, consultants, and doctors discussed the progress of the lady in the bed next to mine, as I listened from the other side of the curtain. I hoped and prayed that our experience would be as positive as hers. She had given birth to a healthy baby girl. With nothing else to occupy my thoughts, I pieced together the details throughout the day as I rested back on the bed. When I was not eavesdropping or sleeping, I listened to music through my headphones. Each time I thought about losing our precious babies, I sobbed until the front of my nightgown was soaked. How I hoped that our season would be one of celebration at the arrival of three healthy babies.

The new mother seemed nervous about breastfeeding, but the midwives were patient and encouraging. The crying baby set me off in tears several times throughout the day and night. After the many visits to the lavatory, I found it difficult to put myself back to sleep, even though I was exhausted. Memories of the voices of the doctors and midwives outlining the worse outcome for us flooded my mind.

Visits from Ash lasted for a few hours as we continued to wait for results regarding our situation. I instantly felt better, stronger, and happier when he was near. The medical staff recommended that I rest in hospital until there were more positive changes in my body.

Grateful for the morning, I read for hours, falling asleep intermittently. Struggling to keep my thoughts going in a positive direction, I tried to drown them out by listening to music. I forced myself to eat the meals provided by the hospital, knowing that I needed to remain nourished and strong. I looked forward to visits from Ash after work because we spent a lot of the time encouraging each other.

After I had been in hospital a couple of days, the doctor visited and reiterated our possible outcomes. He discussed further potential leakage of the amniotic fluid, infection, and going into early labour. I was always uneasy after these discussions; it took me a while to regain my peace of mind. The doctors would prefer that I stay in hospital for at least the next few days. Ash and I talked about our upcoming ultrasound scan on Monday and hoped that all would continue to be well with our babies.

Friday, 31 January 2014

Diary Entry

> The resting has done me a world of good. My leakage issues have subsided, and I have more energy. The midwives are concerned about my circulation, so I am wearing pressure socks on both legs. They aren't the most comfortable or the most attractive accessories, but they will stop me from having any other complications due to lack of movement. The mother who had her baby girl a few days ago left this morning. She was in hospital for this length, as she had a caesarean.

I grew accustomed to hearing that sweet baby cry. Newborns have such a distinct sound. I missed hearing her. I thought about three babies crying at once. *Would each one sound different, or would they have the same tone?* I prayed that we would hear the sweet and piercing cries of our babies in the future.

Most of my time in the ward was spent encouraging myself through worship and scripture. The gospel music lifted my spirit. The lyrics reminded me of God's characteristics and His perspective on our situation. The Bible gave me promises and keys to hang on to. Bathed in worship songs, with an open Bible by my side, I watched the hours come and go.

A family in the same ward had just lost their baby. I heard part of a conversation as I made my way to the bathroom one morning. How devastated they must have felt. I said a prayer for them.

Rest made a huge difference. The doctor visited my bed in the evening with good news. They examined me and gave me the option of returning home to rest. Ash and I listened as the doctor explained my progress. If our situation remained the same, things could be fine.

After six days in hospital, I was ready to return home. It was difficult to sleep easily in there, so Ash and I opted for me to go home.

Peace greeted me when I returned home. The weekend was a continuation of naps and rests. My belly felt tight, and I was not sure why it was difficult for me to stay in one position for very long, but I reminded myself that I was at home and rest would make all the difference.

Monday, 3 February 2014

Diary Entry

> Ash has taken me to hospital early this morning, as we
> have an appointment for our twenty-week ultrasound
> scan.

The orderly ushered us to the radiology department and gestured
towards the waiting room. Our turn arrived, and Ash wheeled
me into the examining room. I propped myself carefully onto the
bed. The lights were dim, and the radiologist checked that I was
comfortable and ready to begin.

Totally captivated by the first sight of our first baby's profile, I
could tell that this was going to be an emotional time. A frequent
visitor to ultrasounds, I was surprised at just how much seeing this
gorgeous outline affected me. The baby moved his arm in a waving
motion, and my heart was overjoyed. This was our baby. I decided
in my heart that I would not allow anyone to take this child or
his siblings away from me. My heart leapt into my throat when I
saw our second child move. Then the third made me smile, again
through tears. It was harder to get an accurate view of our third
baby because of his position in my belly. I could not contain the
affection I felt for each one of them when I saw their tiny profiles,
heads, and appendages. Ash sat staring at the screen with tears in
the corners of his eyes. I reached out my hand towards him. He
clasped my hand in his. This was a very special moment for us—
seeing our three beautiful children. The radiologist told us that
triplets one and two were boys but concluded that determining
the gender of the third baby was going to be too difficult for this
session.

As I was staring at the ultrasound printouts of our babies, my
emotions got the better of me. I thought that I had cried out all

my tears for that day, but somehow seeing them again and feeling them react on the screen moved me profoundly. I did not want to lose them. I said another desperate prayer for our three children.

Ash and I had an appointment with the obstetrician after our ultrasound scan, and she was pleased with the improvements in my condition in the last few days. The symptoms of early labour had almost completely stopped. Ash had to work that afternoon, so my in-laws picked me up. I longed for the comfort and familiarity of home. Feeling confident after a consultation with the hospital, I rested back at home on the couch with a vegetable pasty in my hand. A few bites in, I started to feel as if a vice was gripping my belly. Ash was now at work, so I called my mother-in-law and asked her to come into our lounge room to sit with me as I called the hospital. The tightening became more intense and more frequent. Ash raced home and drove me back to the hospital, as I was in extreme pain.

I groaned constantly as Ash drove us to the hospital. I was readmitted into the ward after being examined and was told that I would have another scan in due time. The medical team appeared calm, but my anxiety shot to new heights with every ounce of pain. I lay back on the bed in the examining room and closed my eyes. Fearing the worst but hoping for the best, I swallowed hard and looked up at the ceiling. I became angry that I was back in hospital again. I could not understand why our journey to becoming parents had taken this detour. I did not accept that we were facing the possibility of losing our precious gifts from God. I was determined in my heart that I would not let go of these children.

Ash and I spent the night in a double-bed suite, which we found out later was generally reserved for parents who appeared to be losing their babies. I was exhausted both physically and emotionally, and my memory of that night is vague. Interruptions to our sleep came in the form of midwives checking my vital signs. The medical staff seemed satisfied with their checks, but I slept with a heavy, anxious heart.

With the morning came reprieve, as Ash and I were moved out of the suite and back into a room in the ward. This transfer boosted our confidence that our babies would be safe and sound, and that we may have escaped the threat of preterm labour. Sustaining my energy with a few morsels of hospital food, I was determined to stay strong and to nourish my body for our boys' sake. Resting on the bed as the hours passed, I tried to remain positive.

That evening, exhaustion overtook me and my body was aching. I reasoned that it must be the hard hospital bed that was making me so uncomfortable. Unfortunately, the symptoms of preterm labour had begun again. I was moved to another area of the hospital in a wheelchair. Throughout the night, I struggled in pain. The midwives said that I was in labour, but I would not accept it. With each contraction, I struggled to stay still, but I would not let go of my children. My whole body shook in the bed as I cried out to God for help. *Why was He not answering my prayer for this all to stop?* My only comfort was that Ash was by my side.

And then it happened. My waters broke. That signalled the end.

I was immediately moved to the birthing suite. Anxiety enveloped me like an unwelcome heavy blanket. I froze but prayed harder. My whole body tensed up, and I was determined that this would not be the end of our children's lives. The birthing suite room was dark, and as we entered the room I glanced across at the trays of instruments. After being lifted onto the bed by the midwives, I lay on my back, looking up at the darkened roof. My eyes took a while to focus on the glints of light coming from outside the room. The pain continued, and the contractions absorbed my strength. Totally helpless, I used my waning strength to hold on to my babies.

My head swirled with desperate thoughts. I begged and cried out to God in whispered prayer. I asked Him to do a miracle. I believed that He could. My thoughts raced wildly through my mind while the midwives moved around the room.

Writhing in pain, I held on to my belly and drew my legs together. One of the midwives gently touched my leg and encouraged me to allow the birthing to proceed. I moaned and began to cry, but I eventually gave in to her request. My thoughts raged on. It seemed as though I had entered a nightmare and needed to wake up to stop this horror from happening. I cried out and groaned, but it was no use. Our first baby crowned.

In the panic and pain, my desperation peaked. An ache began in my heart, and I felt completely powerless. The midwives called for me to push, but that was the last thing I wanted to do. I longed to get up off the bed and run out of the room.

Despite the chaos in my mind and the ache in my heart, I knew God was in the room, because He said that He would never leave me. Even so, I was terrified.

Finally I released my control, breathed out, and whispered, 'I trust you, God.'

Our first son was born. There was no cry—no sound at all.

Our second son was born much the same as the first.

I began to sob from a deep place.

Our third son was born. There was silence.

I scrunched up my face in pain as the tears rolled down the sides of my face.

Emptiness filled the room. There were soft noises coming from the midwives as they continued their job. I lay still, shocked and void. My eyes closed, I prayed that this was just a dream—a nightmare. I lied to myself that when I opened my eyes it would all be as it was before. I longed to be back in my bed at home in the dark room, just looking at the iridescent alarm clock digits. Heaviness settled over me, and I could not cry any more. The ache grew inside my heart. For a moment, a fleeting thought passed by me. This unwelcome thought appeared and then disappeared several times over the next few minutes.

Let me die too.

As if awakened from a daydream, I shook the thought away. Something rose within. I would not give in to that evil thought. I would not allow myself to be dragged down into a pit of gloom. I had dealt with those thoughts many years ago and drew the line back when I was twelve years old. Back then those tempting thoughts were my daily torments; they were there to greet me in the early hours of the morning, and they hovered over me in my bed at night. That part of my life had been dealt with. A divine man who loved me and rescued me dealt with this issue centuries before I was born. He died in my place so that I did not have to face death alone and so I could have hope, a future, and eternal life.

The evil invitation for death was not able to tempt me because God's redemptive love was in my heart. Thankful for my relationship with God, I tried to listen for His voice. I focused on the tiles of the hospital room ceiling, and I cleared my mind.

I carefully followed each edge of the tile across from one corner of the ceiling and back. This inane task helped to distract my thoughts from spiralling into an abyss of pain.

Ash painfully recollected seeing one of the boys' hands stretched out as the nurse carried him away to clean him straight after he had been born.

As the boys were born, the midwives wrapped them in tiny blankets, gave each baby a small woollen beanie, and placed them in Ash's arms. He prayed over them and told them that Mummy and Daddy loved them very much. At one point when the nurses left the room, Ash sang over our babies, tears streaming from his eyes. The few lines that he sang were from a song I wrote for my father when he passed away.

> You are safe in His arms
>
> I know you're okay
>
> You are free
>
> To fly again
>
> I see your smiling faces
>
> (Taken from the song 'You Are Free', from the album *Photo Album* by Digital Prophets 2003)

At some point during this sombre scene, Ash asked me if I wanted to see our boys. In a state of shock and overwhelmed by the whole experience, I could not find the strength I needed, so I told him no.

Our precious, tiny baby boys stayed in Ash's arms for close to an hour, until each one passed away peacefully. As he handed each baby to the nurse, he leaned close and gave each boy one last kiss.

The few hours after giving birth were emotionally dark. My parents-in-law were on their way to the hospital with my mother so that we could share the heartbreaking news with them in person.

Our parents were ushered into the room. I was lying on the bed, covered by a hospital blanket, so they were fully taken by surprise when we announced that our babies had been born prematurely and had been too young to survive. Shock filled the atmosphere in the room. My mother took my hand and suggested that we pray. My mother-in-law, my father-in-law, my mother, Ash, and I spent that moment asking God for help. I had a tangible sense of God's peace resting on me like a warm, protective sheet. Our parents did not stay long, as the midwives needed to examine me.

Later I was moved back to the hospital suite. Ash and I spent the next little while going through the motions of getting settled into the family room. After the midwife took my vital signs, I seized the opportunity to shower. Moving as if in slow motion, I found it hard to speak. I fought off the urge to cry, but every now and then I groaned.

The water was warm and soothing. I sobbed as I rested my forehead against the shower wall and pressed both palms against the cool tiles to support myself. I wept for what seemed like an eternity. My energy was almost completely sapped. My eyes were filled with a mixture of water and salty tears. My throat hurt, my body hurt, my head hurt—everything hurt. I placed my head under the showerhead and allowed the water to run from the top of my head to the tips of my toes. All I could hear was the water dripping down into the drain. The fragrant soap pleasantly cascaded over my body. Then I looked down. I saw that my pregnant belly had changed. It was much smaller than before. I called out and moaned loudly, and I then started to cry again.

Ash tried his best to console me from the other room, but I could tell that he, too, needed comfort. I stood under the shower for a long time as the water washed away every single tear. After crying myself dry, I turned my attention to God. A presence filled the large, cold, empty bathroom. I had experienced this tangible sensation many times before. I knew it was God's presence. In a way, it was as if turning my thoughts towards him broke through the emptiness and eased the ache I began to feel in my heart.

When I was somewhat refreshed from my shower, we settled into the large, comfortable hospital bed and prepared for a long-awaited rest. Only as I placed my head on the pristine white pillow did I realize just how tired I was. It was not long before I was sound asleep.

The next day was filled with more checks. We were cared for by sympathetic, obliging staff that made our day as comfortable as possible. Ash and I settled back and enjoyed a nourishing breakfast as we discussed how we were going to deal with this loss. After much conversation and prayer, and many tears, we decided to let those close to us know about our heartbreak.

During our time in hospital, we rested and prayed. We comforted each other and encouraged each other by talking through what we were feeling, but we decided not to ask why. We asked God to heal our broken hearts, to bring some good out of this tragedy, and to restore joy to us again. The hospital staff had been particularly kind and sensitive in the way they were interacting with us each time they visited our room to check on my recovery. They could not have been kinder, but I felt worse as reality set in. We received texts from loved ones who had been informed, which helped us get through the dark hours of the day as we grieved the loss of our precious triplet babies.

Friday, 7 February 2014

<u>Diary Entry</u>

> Our beautiful triplet baby boys went home to heaven
> on Wednesday at 4.30 a.m. As they arrived, I told God
> that I trust Him. Ash and I named them Summer, Snow,
> and Sky so that we will always have reminders of them
> throughout our lives. This was one of the hardest things
> to accept, but God is good whether we understand His
> ways or not. It really hurts. I am broken-hearted. I truly
> hoped and believed that they would live.

We were told that we would be discharged from the hospital
in the morning. To further add insult to injury, Ash and I had
purchased a car specifically for our triplets, and Friday was the
day we had organized to pick it up. Although our situation had
taken a devastating turn for the worse, we decided to honour
our commitment to buying the car. We discussed how we could
manage picking it up that morning. Ash was rostered to go to
work, and we decided that it would be best if he went, as it would
be a welcome distraction from the raw, tender situation we were
in. I was planning on sleeping for most of the day, so it made sense
for Ash to drive straight to work after picking up our new car.

Ash informed the car salesman that we had been dealing with
of the loss of our boys and asked if he would be as prompt and
discreet as possible, in light of our changed circumstances. Signing
the papers and collecting keys for our new car should have been
an event of excitement, but instead it was one of the most joyless
transactions we had ever experienced.

I left Ash to organize the new car, and as I set out for home on my
own, I cried uncontrollably. A heavy blanket of emotion settled
over me as I turned out of the dealership car park. The ache

returned, and a fireball of rage rose from within my chest and came out through my mouth. Even though Ash and I had agreed to grieve well, I could not contain my anger in that moment. I cried and screamed wildly as I drove. Every part of my body was shaking with fury. I could barely hold on to the steering wheel and even thought that I should stop the car and wait until this heated episode passed, but just as I tried to find a place to pull over, I saw a woman walking her child in a pram along the side of the road. My eyes flooded with tears, making it difficult to see where I was going, and I began to sob. I eventually turned into the driveway of our home and turned the car off. Then, deflated and weak, I rested my head on the steering wheel and allowed the tears to flow freely. Negative thoughts swamped my mind. Questions rose and assaulted my peace. *How could this have happened? What did I do wrong? How could we have saved them? Is there any hope of us ever having children who live?*

Being home made the reality of our loss hit hard. The gloomy thought struck me like a punch in my chest: I was here without our babies. I felt emptiness in my heart as I rubbed my hand over my void belly. They were gone. My babies were no longer with me. This wretched pain brought nothing but tears. Doubt filled me as I considered what I had done to cause this. I wished, longed, and was desperate to go to sleep to erase the whole memory and wake up pregnant again. How could I escape this misery? I would never again complain about my sore back or legs. I promised not to make a big deal about my nausea. I would rest more. I would pray more. *What could I do to change what had happened? How could I get my precious babies back?*

Like a clay statue, I sat in the driveway for a long time. I am not sure how long I sat there, but it was long enough that my tears dried up, just as my soul felt dried up. The memory of the aftermath of the births in hospital revisited my thoughts repeatedly. After listening for a long while to some birds twittering in a nearby tree, I reluctantly lifted my body out of the car and walked into the house. My parents-in-law had kindly removed every memorable trace of the preparations, gifts, and cards for our babies.

As I passed the kitchen, I stopped and looked at the couch in our lounge room. This was the last place I had sat in our home while I was still pregnant. Tears forming in my eyes again, I walked over to the couch and stared down at the seat. Positioning myself in the exact same place I had sat only days before this tragedy, I closed my wet eyes and sobbed. I now felt heavy but hollow. The memory of talking to the midwife from the hospital and timing the cramps as she instructed me to on my phone came to mind. How desperate I had felt in that moment. If only I had known what was to come.

Eventually I dragged myself to my bedroom and sat on our bed, curtains drawn, lights off. I placed my journal and Bible in front of me. I pressed play on my favourite worship album and closed my eyes as I let the music fill my soul. I tried to avoid thinking about what had happened two days before and instead focused on the one who had always been with me—the one who would never leave. The words of the worship song caused the lump in my throat to harden. This hurt. I felt this could break me. Those melodies and words usually brought comfort, but now they were like razors scratching the surface of my exposed and broken heart. My first inclination was to sing along as I had in the past, but my will to sing had left me. *How can I sing of your faithfulness when losing our boys made me question whether or not you are faithful? How can I sing of your love when I feel like you let me down? How can I sing of your goodness, when everything that happened in the past few days showed me the opposite?* Those thoughts caused a storm in my mind. I imagined the thoughts swirling around high and wild, like dry autumn leaves on a windy day. I sat still and continued to listen to the songs without joining in. My posture was rigid, but my heart ached for help. Locked into my anger, I was stuck. I told God I needed help. I threw myself against the mattress and yelled and cried. With clenched fists, I beat the bed and screamed that it wasn't fair. I told God that I wouldn't be able to cope. I was resolute that I would not leave the room until I had help to stop this pain from consuming me. Angry and violent words flew out of my mouth, but the release did not bring the comfort I craved.

With my heart pounding, a mixture of sweat and tears ran across my face. I stopped to hear that God was silent. I heard nothing. The anger had gone, but the hollowness remained. Then I realized that I was demanding help, not asking for it. After a few moments of considering whom I was talking to, I understood that I had no right to demand anything. I was talking to God. I was addressing the King of Kings, the God of the universe, the Almighty. *Who was I to address Him in this manner?* He was also my Heavenly Father, who had shown nothing but love, acceptance, mercy, peace, and kindness from the very beginning.

He had rescued me many, many times in the past. I thought of how He taught me to see myself as beautiful. I remembered how He brought people into my life that loved me, helped me, comforted me, taught me, and blessed me. I recalled the words that He had spoken to me, the opportunities He had given me, and the gifts He had showered me with. I considered the pictures that He had shared with me and the visions of things to come. I recollected His voice. That voice was like no other. I reminisced on how I used to be before I met Him and how I changed because of Him. I remembered His mercy on my life and how I could have remained rejected and abandoned, but He chose to rescue me. My heart melted as I remembered.

I opened my Bible.

'He heals the broken hearted and binds up their wounds' (Psalm 147:3 NIV).

I told God that I believed those words. The tears flowed from my eyes, and I began to sob. Something welled up from deep within, and I groaned. It was an excruciating, mournful groan. It was the type of cry that comes from that hidden, dark place of loss. And it was uncontrollable. I wept for the loss of our precious boys. I offered myself back into His care and asked for help as I humbled myself to His will.

Suddenly I sensed a release, and then my pain was replaced with an overwhelmingly hopeful peace. It is hard to describe exactly what that peace felt like, but it was what I needed in that moment. My soul drank it in like a weary plant in a scorching, dusty desert.

The music played on, and I listened to the words and the sweet melody. Rocking gently to the beat, I felt as if I were a child being held by her singing parent. The peace settled in me, around me, behind me, and in front of me. I could breathe again. I felt relaxed and calm. This was God's holy presence. He had come to meet me in my pain, in my pit of despair. He was near. I opened my journal and began to write.

Diary Entry

> I see an image in my mind's eye of a doorway. Three young boys are standing in front of me. They are all wearing short-sleeved shirts and shorts. One boy is wearing a blue shirt, one is wearing a white shirt, and the third is wearing a yellow-and-blue-striped shirt. We are all looking through the frame of this doorway into paradise. It is no place like I have ever seen before. It's a perfect place, with green trees, stunningly gorgeous flowers, and lush green grass. The colours are vibrant and

amazing. Looking through the doorway at this utopia, I feel sad. I begin to cry because I can't step through the doorway to enter that beautiful place with my boys, but I need to say goodbye. Two of the boys run ahead into this beautiful place. They run away. They leave me and run through the doorway and onto a path leading up a green hill with luscious, thick emerald grass. I quickly grab the last boy at the doorway and try to stop him from going any further. I wrestle with him. My arms are wrapped around him, and I hold him tight. He struggles for a while but makes no sound. "I can't let you go," I whisper into his ear. My voice is thick with emotion. He doesn't say anything. I can't see his face or hear his voice, but I hold on even tighter. Then I look up through the doorway. The two other boys are standing on the top of the hill in the distance, and Jesus is standing with them. Jesus smiles at me. I know that they are safe with Jesus. I know that He will take care of them. Through tears, I kiss the top of my boy's curly mop of hair, and I release him. He runs away. The doorway vanishes, and I open my eyes.

In that moment I was reminded that we are living on one side of eternity. One day I would be reunited with our boys, but for now we were apart. Believing that life was temporary and that an eternal life awaited us brought my soul the tonic it needed. I looked down at my journal, scribbled down the details of this vision, and opened my Bible to Jeremiah 18. This verse stood out on the page: '… so the potter formed it into another pot, shaping it as seemed best to him' (Jeremiah 18:4 NIV). I recalled God showing this story to me a while ago. I felt as if He was preparing me for this change.

My faith in a loving God who never meant for death, pain, loss, and other catastrophes to be part of our lives, was what was holding me together. A choice made in a garden back in the beginning left us all susceptible to the effects of brokenness, disease, pain, and loss. I knew that I was imperfect and this world that I live in is blemished and flawed. Dreadful things happen to many people. Injustices, cruelty, hatred, abuses, and many other atrocities are rife. Even so, I had a choice to make. I could get caught up in the unfairness and horror of the situation, or I could look to the only one who could help restore my shattered and broken heart.

My conversation with God continued in the vein of love and trust. It dawned on me that I could never say that I truly loved God until I showed that I trusted Him, because 'it (love) always trusts' (1 Corinthians 13:6 NIV).

Diary Entry

> I have a sense that this tragic situation has the potential to make Ash and me stronger. We need to mourn for our boys. We show God that we trust Him by accepting His healing, by continuing to be hopeful, and by being softhearted towards Him. We show Him that we love Him by the trust that we place in Him. We show the Potter that our lives are truly in His hands and that He is free to make decisions that seem best to Him.

Control was a huge issue in my life. I was now at a point where I had to make a choice. I thought back through the dark and devastating times in my life (which involved abuse, family violence, addictions, and other things that come in the package of brokenness). Sometimes I chose to hold on to the anger, bitterness and pain when things went wrong. I refused to release any of it into God's hands, so I suffered a lot as I tried to do it all by myself. However, when I chose to trust God, I still experienced some of the pain of the situation, the loss, the injustice, and the disaster, but He was with me to help me through. He was the only one who could truly heal and restore me. He alone could release me and set me free to move ahead.

I read a passage in the book of Romans: 'And we know that in all things God works for the good of those who love him, who have been called according to his purpose' (Romans 8:28 NIV).

Ash and I later discussed the revelation God had given me. We were not going to let this loss take any more from us. With God's help, we could see something good come out of it.

Saturday, 8 February 2014

Diary Entry

> Each day, I focus on my routine. The medical team warned me about postnatal depression. Desperate not to add to our pain, I ask God to help me. I keep strong and positive by organizing my day in hour blocks. I am healing well physically after giving birth, and I should be able to start walking around the park again soon. I am reading a helpful book called *Good Grief* by Granger Westberg.

After Ash arrived home from work, we discussed our future plans. We usually engaged in those types of conversations at the starts of new seasons in our lives. Ash and I agreed that our time should be spent together, with family and friends, on building our health, and in helping others. I expressed the desire to return to work casually in the near future.

I spent time thinking about how people rebuild their cities after natural disasters, tragedies, or terrorist attacks. *How do they start? When all hope fades, how are they able to believe in a bright future again? How do they deal with the void that the loss leaves in its wake?* I considered the millions of other people around the world who had far greater struggles and challenges to deal with each day.

I was not under the pressure or in the dire circumstances to have to find my next dollar or next meal. I was well taken care of and had no trouble with meeting my basic physical needs each day. I was not under immediate attack for my gender, race, or religion. I had not been captured or enslaved. I was free to live with the convictions in my heart. Of course, I was not minimizing our loss, but in the scheme of things, I had hope and help to get through this life-changing heartbreaking situation.

Snuggled under the covers, I began thinking about the day ahead. My ears tuned in to the magpies singing sweetly outside my bedroom window. Ash's cologne still filled the air of the room hours after he had left for work. The comfort of the smooth sheets over my legs and the mattress firmly supporting my body enticed me to stay in bed for a while longer. The dark, heavy thoughts visited me every morning as I opened my eyes. It was a choice to get out of bed. It was a decision to take care of myself. My conviction that God would bring good out of this tragedy kept me going each day. The lure of self-pity, anger, and bitterness was there every morning, knocking on the door of my heart and mind, but I would not allow them in. I trained my thoughts to stay on the positive path, and when the bandits of negativity surprised me on the road, I fought them off with promises from the Bible for my life and moved on.

I had the sense that God wanted me to return to what I was doing before I became pregnant. I was working part-time, completing my counselling degree, songwriting, volunteering at our church, and writing story ideas.

I read Psalm 37 this morning: 'The Lord makes firm the steps of the one who delights in him' (Psalm 37:23 NIV).

My mother and youngest brother came to our home for a visit. We had afternoon tea together and chatted for a few hours. My brother had some errands to run, so my mother stayed back to chat further with me. I explained that God's presence had completely surrounded us in hospital. It was the most difficult situation that Ash and I had faced as a couple, but we believed that we were recipients of God's supernatural help and were supported by the love and prayers of our family and friends.

My parents-in-law and I watched the Sochi Winter Olympics together. Ash worked in the evenings, so they kept me company until he got home. Grief can be a lonely process. I did not like being on my own for too long during those first few days. My negative thoughts gained energy from isolation. I began to ruminate on destructive paths of thinking when I was alone. However, when there were others around me to distract me from those bad thoughts, I was able to keep my mind in a positive frame.

Our family and close friends had been a wonderful support to us. We received meals and encouraging messages throughout the day. I knew that many people thought of us and prayed for us. In a way, I felt as if Ash and I were in a cocoon of love created by our community. It was safe here, and we were under no pressure to leave this cocoon until we were ready.

Each day I chose a song or a few songs to listen to, wrote in my journal, did some light chores, and started walking around our local park. Intense and sudden loss certainly refocused me to the priorities in life.

Monday, 10 February 2014

<u>Diary Entry</u>

The ache of what we are planning on doing today just won't go away. I haven't been able to eat breakfast because this is weighing heavy on me. I feel ill at the thought that only a little while ago we posted the good news of our boys, and now, in such a short time, everything has changed. Today we will post our sad news. It doesn't seem fair that we had them in our lives only for such a short time. I had a good cry before chatting with Ash this morning. We decided on when to let our wider community know of our loss.

In a Facebook post, we wrote the following:

It is with sadness that we let you know that our three lovely boys Summer, Snow, and Sky were born and then went to be with God a short time later last Wednesday morning. We are okay and have a peace in our hearts that God is looking after them. Thank you to all those who have sent kind words of encouragement and condolences. Your words have helped to begin the healing process. For people thinking that they might send flowers, they are welcome to, but we would appreciate the thought just as much if instead they could donate via us to Orphancare Foundation. We will be sending a lump sum to Orphancare in Cape Town in March in memory of our boys. At least our loss can in some way add life to some children who don't have parents or have been abandoned.

Thanks—Ash and Liesl

<u>Diary Entry</u>

Ash and I have had an outpouring of encouragement from our friends and wider community. We read the comments as they come in, which has helped us in the healing process. We are grateful that we are part of such a loving village.

Tuesday, 11 February 2014

Diary Entry

Thank you God for a wonderful sleep. I feel well rested.
The weather is cooler. It's a new day—a new beginning:
a fresh start filled with hope and purpose.

I carefully jotted down the details on a notepad as I listened to the voice on the phone relay my steps for re-entering my counselling course. The counselling coordinator had been kind, helpful, and sensitive to my needs. I ended the conversation feeling hopeful.

Helping others had always been a priority and an enjoyable part of my life, from the time I used to volunteer at my church during my teenage years, to the recent work we did in Cape Town.

Diary Entry

Ash and I booked our tickets for our trip to South Africa
yesterday. I'm excited because it is only five weeks and
two days away. We will be leaving in March.

If you had told me that I would be travelling back to South Africa year after year, I would not have believed you. I love the country of my birth and seeing my relatives and friends there, but three trips in three years was definitely unexpected. There was something about Cape Town that kept calling us back. We love the people, the landscape, the community, the food, and the spirit of the place. People we know in Cape Town know the value of hard work and seem to be grateful for everything they have, yet they are extremely generous. We've met many beautiful souls who have pressed through unimaginable difficulties and are now living to help others.

Wednesday, 12 February 2014

This morning I woke up at 4.00 a.m. I spent the next hour and a half writing a song in honour of our triplets.

> Calling
>
> Heaven was calling
> Calling you
> True to the promise
> Love will embrace me through
> And I live in hope
> That someday
> I will see you
> Heaven was calling
> His voice was calling you, little darling
>
> V1
> Waiting patiently
> I dreamed of what could be
> On the day I'd see your face
> Not a sound you made
> When you went away
> You drifting peacefully into Love
> Heaven was calling
> Calling you
> True to the promise
> Love will embrace me through
> And I live in hope
> The One who cares
> will always be there
> Heaven was calling
> His voice was calling you, little darling

(Lyrics taken from 'Calling' by L. A. Field, 2014)

Thursday, 13 February

Diary Entry

> Ash contacted Bethel Funeral Services to arrange for
> the boys' bodies to be cremated. The thought of them in
> a tiny coffin is painful. We are meeting with the funeral
> director today at our home.

I heard a knock on the door and braced myself as I opened to a
friendly face. The funeral director came to help us sort through the
paperwork of our boys' cremation. She was patient and sensitive—
perfect for her role in helping people put loved ones to rest. After
the intensity of discussing details of their death and plans for their
cremation, Ash and I were overcome with emotion.

Diary Entry

> Ash and I had a cry and then ate some vegemite
> sandwiches and fruit together. We drove to Chelsea
> beach and watched the calmness of the water from the
> car. We sat in silence for most of the time, until sunset.
> The weather was grey and hazy but peaceful—a good
> representation of our current moods.

We have decided to keep one set of the baby's clothing gifts because
we have hope that God will bless us with at least one more child.

A school friend of Ash's wrote us a poem. This kind of artistic
expression had a unique way of helping to paint the emotional
pictures that our hearts were experiencing. I was grateful for
the therapeutic balm that poetry, songwriting, and therapeutic
conversations brought in this season.

Today I read something else that brought me comfort and peace. 'When my heart was grieved and my spirit embittered. I was senseless and ignorant. Yet I am always with you. You hold me by my right hand. You guide me with your counsel and afterward, you will take me into glory' (Psalm 73:21–26 NIV).

People were amazed at Ash's and my attitude during this grieving period. Many that we had spoken to commented on the peace and even joy they witnessed in us despite our devastating loss. Ash and I possessed an advantage in our grieving process. We believed in an afterlife. Our faith, based on the Holy Bible, reassured us that we were eternal beings. We knew that death was not the end. Perhaps it felt like it, but we believed that death was a transition from this life to the new one. We believed that once our spirits left our bodies, we would enter peace. This reassurance that our faith in God brought was essential for moving forward through grief. We had a hopeful perspective of loss and death. Understanding that there was a purpose in every one of life's situations, we were able to make meaning of our loss and work through it as well as we possibly could. We accepted that life is not perfect and that bad things happen to all of us, but we were convinced that we would all be in perfect peace and joy in heaven one day. The comfort that the Bible brought was priceless. It was when I was at my lowest that I truly needed someone, something, to depend on. The experience of going through a twenty-week pregnancy and then giving birth to those precious babies only to lose them was enough to send anyone into depression. However, because of my faith and my belief in a higher power, yet a personal God, I had access to hope and peace through one of the most difficult storms I had ever encountered.

Friday, 14 February 2014

As I sat on our bed and wrote my thoughts in my journal for the day, I was interrupted by another God whisper. 'Go ahead and move forward. Busy yourself with loving people and living out what I have called you to do.'

After pondering those words for a while, I continued to write in my journal.

<u>Diary Entry</u>

> I will not lose faith or hope. God is bigger than any disappointment, obstacle or doubt!

I meditated on the promises of the Bible in the book of Ephesians.

'We are God's handiwork, created in Christ Jesus to do good works, which God prepared in advance for us to do' (Ephesians 2:10 NIV). Those kinds of encouragements were always nourishing to my soul. I couldn't give up, because there was a purpose for me.

My best friend was truly a gift from God. I could not believe that we had been friends for over seventeen years. The strange thing is that before I knew her well, she did not seem like anyone who would want to be my friend. She and her family attended the same church as my parents, grandmother and other relatives. I used to go along to some Sunday-morning services with the ulterior motive of enjoying my grandmother's roast potatoes for Sunday lunch afterward. In the early days of our friendship, I recalled feeling as though we had been friends for years. Since then I have been blessed by her kindness, sense of humour, generosity, and faithfulness.

Tuesday, 18 February 2014

<u>Diary Entry</u>

> I had a pretty miserable afternoon, so I went to bed early.
> I read for a while and then eventually went to sleep. I
> am struggling with my thought life. My mind keeps
> drifting to unpleasant thoughts. I have been aggressive
> and moody for most of today. I am feeling listless and
> bored. I just want to give up. I feel as if we are right back
> where we were last year. Every year in the same place.
> We aren't moving forward in life. It feels as if we are just
> running on a treadmill, not going anywhere.
>
> God, where are you? Can you hear me? I'm so tired; I
> need you to help me. I'm sinking. My soul is in anguish.

After a few moments of waiting for a reply, I placed my journal
on the bed and walked out of our bedroom. The kettle boiled,
and I stared at the steam rising quickly as it began to whistle. As
I poured the hot water into the cup and thought about how I had
been unable to drink tea during my pregnancy with the triplets,
my emotions overwhelmed me. In many ways, I had returned
to my normal way of living. If only this ache in my heart would
leave. If only the thoughts that dragged me down each day would
dissolve. If only I would be able to let go of 'what could have been'.

Something occurred to me from out of nowhere; the discomfort
I was experiencing could be linked to something from my past
coming back to haunt me—to hurt me. I could not put my finger
on it.

As I carefully navigated my way back to our bedroom with a full
cup in hand, I had an epiphany. I felt abandoned. I felt as if God
had abandoned me in the birthing suite in hospital. I knew that He
loved me and had promised never to leave me, but for a moment in

that birthing suite, I felt as if I were alone. I knew I was at another crossroads. *Was I going to rely solely on my emotions about what had happened, or would I rely on what I knew was true?* The fact was that we had lost our babies and God had not allowed them to live. I believed that He was the giver of life and it was at His call that a person lived or died. We prayed, we believed, we hoped, and we confessed, but they still died. I may not have understood it all from this perspective, and God was not angry with me because I tried and failed to, but if I was to live with any kind of peace, I needed to realize that all I could do was trust the goodness of His character. The Bible told me that God would never leave me. The Bible told me that He had good plans for my life. The Bible said that God was a good Father with good gifts. The Bible said that if I trusted Him, past my own understanding, He would make my paths straight.

These thoughts hovered over my mind like a moth around a flame. I had a choice to make. *Would I allow that doubt and mistrust to taint my belief in a trustworthy God, or would I believe that although I had suffered this loss, God was with me and did not leave me for one second? Would I look at my situation from my own wounded, fragile perspective, or would I look at it through the way I imagined God saw it? Would I resign myself to living without any hope for the future, or would I trust God to walk us through this and on to a hopeful, happy future?*

I contemplated for a while and busied myself writing in my journal.

Diary Entry

> I whispered in that hospital room when our boys entered the world, 'I still trust you, Lord.' I know you know best. I will keep going. I will prove to you that I trust you in the way I behave. I choose to be content, at peace, and joyfully expectant.

Wednesday, 19 February 2014

Diary Entry

> It has been two weeks since our baby boys went to heaven.
> My heart is still hurting.

I closed the door after climbing out of the car and looked out over the partially empty car park. Ash and I had frequented this cluster of shops many times from the days of dating through to years later into our marriage. We walked aimlessly through the department store and looked at the various items of interest. I deliberately avoided walking past the baby aisle and felt a twinge of sadness as my eyes drifted towards a shelf displaying baby wipes, bath products, and bibs at the end of the aisle.

Laden with purchased items that we would probably never use, we exited the shop and headed towards the supermarket. I smiled at the pregnant lady that passed us. *How lucky she is*, I thought to myself. She looked beautiful and motherly with a large ball-shaped package on the front of her petite body. Dark rings around the lower parts of her eyes and the way she waddled slowly next to her partner made me believe that she was close to her due date. *That was me only a few weeks ago*, I thought sadly. *Would I ever feel happy for other parents who were allowed to keep their babies to full term and beyond?* My mind was not in a good space.

That night in bed, I struggled to fall asleep. I decided to get up and write in my journal, which usually helped me to decipher what was going on in my heart and mind.

Mid-thought, I stopped writing when I heard God whisper, 'Try again.'

'No,' I whispered back.

'Try again,' the voice repeated.

I felt the emotion in my chest rise. My eyes filled with tears, and I wiped them away angrily.

'No,' I said more audibly.

There was silence, and I allowed the tears to flow.

After discussing this with Ash in the morning, he encouraged me to listen to God. I knew that neither God nor Ash would pressure me to do anything that would be detrimental for my physical or mental health, but this was a hard pill to swallow. Trying to become pregnant again once my body had recovered felt like one of the most difficult things. I wrestled with the idea of trusting again, of losing my heart again, and of building up my hope only to have it dashed into a million pieces. It felt too early. It felt too hard. It felt impossible.

Doubts whirled around in my head as I sat and stared out of the lounge room window later in the day. I adjusted myself on the couch and decided to think about something else. I focused my attention on the plans for our upcoming mini holiday that a few of our kind friends had organized for us. As I was busily selecting the clothing I would take, my mind took a little rest from it all. Still not back to my normal wardrobe, I looked for a few loose items that would fit comfortably.

Gratitude usually got me back on a positive track in my thoughts and feelings, so I decided to spend the rest of my time thinking about the things in my life that I could be grateful for. I was truly overwhelmed by the kindness and generosity lavished on us by our family and friends. Recounting these things, I thought of the many gifts and meals we had received since we arrived home from the hospital, as well as the many messages that had come by mail, on Facebook, and via texts, all proving to us how much we were loved. Ash and I were grateful for the trip to Torquay, which was gifted to us by a group of friends. While we were on our holiday, we made it a priority to read through a few messages together daily. It was amazing how therapeutic this practice had become. Those words from our loved ones brought healing, strength, peace, and laughter.

The dark moments of my day didn't last for very long, and I fought the urge to ruminate on the negative memories of our hospital experience. I was not avoiding the thoughts completely, but I chose when and how I would think about them. I believed that I was in control of my own thoughts.

Thursday, 27 February 2014

Diary Entry

> I read through the book of Ruth in the Bible a few times yesterday (Ruth chapters1–4 in the NIV). Ruth had lost her husband, security, future hopes, dreams, financial support, role and identity in the community, companion, and chance to have a family. Then, because Naomi decided to leave Moab, Ruth almost lost her remaining in-law and link to her late husband. Ruth could have given up and become depressed or left Naomi to fend for herself, but she chose to have a humble attitude and a heart willing to help, and not give up because the circumstances were bad. Because Ruth chose to have a hopeful attitude, because she never gave up caring for those around her and worked steadily, God chose to honour her life and memory by making her King David's great-grandmother and an ancestor of Jesus Christ.

It was difficult to think that our situation would be dissimilar. It would take a miracle. *I knew God was able to do the impossible, but would He? Was biological parenthood actually part of His plan for Ash and me?* Time would tell. I focused on getting through the moments, hours, or days ahead. Further than that, I did not have space in my mind for anything else. My mind swirled with questions about what this next season could bring. *Would I fall pregnant again this soon? Did I dare hope again?*

I yielded my will to God's will.

Summer, Snow and Sky in Ash's arms.

3

AUTUMN BLUES

Sunday, 2 March 2014

<u>Diary Entry</u>

> I read an encouraging scripture this morning: 'We plan the way we want to live, but only God makes us able to live it' (Proverbs 16:9 MSG). It is a new month, and with it comes a fresh new start!

After starting the day well, I found my enthusiasm waning. I grumbled about how all I'd ever wanted in my life was to have a happy family, after growing up in a dysfunctional home. How naive I was in thinking that getting married and starting a life with someone I loved would finally allow this dream to come to pass. Never did I consider that Ash and I would have our own obstacles to face.

As I became angry and started to cry, I heard God whisper, 'I'm not finished with you yet.'

It was so clear that it shocked me out of my miserable state. I wiped my face and sat up on the bed. *Could this really be only part of our story? Would we have another chapter? Would this chapter include a baby of our own?*

Writing in my journal, I tried to organize my thoughts. I had read somewhere that gratitude was the antidote for complaining. For the past few days, I had felt like complaining about many different things. Angry most evenings, I found myself getting upset, but I was not sure why. Intense emotional episodes convinced me that I could be having a mental breakdown, but as soon as I spoke to someone about how I was feeling, I noticed the power of negativity dissipate.

A recorded list of what I was grateful for in my life helped realign my thinking and focus. The list was long, and I could continue for many pages in my journal. I decided to stop at ten things and committed to work on this list every day that week.

My counselling placement at the aged care home was scheduled to begin in June. At the pre-counselling placement meeting, the supervisor was personable, and she instantly put me at ease. When the idea of looking for a counselling placement to continue my counselling course came to mind, I was hesitant. Considering what the start of this year had been like, I thought that I would be too vulnerable to be helping others. However, June gave me a few months to prepare myself. After meeting the supervisor, I was excited about the prospect of working with those precious elderly residents.

Friday, 14 March 2014

After dropping Ash at the Grand Prix for work, I had a little cry in the car. Negative emotions started to creep back in, but I forced myself not to give in. Convinced that tears could bring healing, I allowed mine to flow.

Memories took me back to those childhood years of suffering with tension and violence in our home. Powerless, I longed for a different life—a peaceful home. God was with me in the misery and chose to rescue me from that situation eventually.

Now I was living in a peaceful, secure home, and if God could change my life in such a dramatic way, what was stopping me from believing that He could do it again? After all, didn't I believe, and hadn't I referred to Him as the God of the impossible?

While I was praying this morning, I saw an image. It was of Ash and me sitting on a large white couch, with two children climbing over us. We were all having fun and laughing.

Sunday, 16 March 2014

<u>Diary Entry</u>

> This verse always brings me comfort: 'When you pass through the waters, I will be with you; and when you pass through the rivers they will not sweep over you. When you walk through the fire, you will not be burned the flames will not set you ablaze' (Isaiah 43:1–3 NIV).

Ash and I had a chat once he got home. He encouraged me not to be worried about the meeting on Monday with the hospital. It was scheduled to discuss what happened with the triplets.

Nursing a cup of hot tea in my hand, I stared out over the balcony of our front porch. I began to sense anxiety sneaking its way into my thoughts and feelings about this meeting with the doctors at the hospital. It would be the first time that we were back in that place since we lost our boys. Unsure of how I would cope, I defaulted to my belief that unpleasant things or fearful situations could be good for me, because they allowed my courage to rise within. I asked God for help.

Tuesday, 18 March 2014

<u>Diary Entry</u>

> God, please help us today as we go into the hospital for this meeting. It is my usual manner to avoid uncomfortable, awkward situations that I have no control of, but today I cannot avoid this appointment. God, if you don't help me, I don't know if I can cope.

Nervously adjusting my skirt, I slowed my breathing and tried to relax. The last time we were in this waiting room, I was pregnant. I looked around at the expectant mothers as they slowly took their seats. A lady next to us was snacking on a mandarin. The sweet scent of the fruit rose to my nose, and I instinctively wiped the back of my hand across my nose to try to avoid the smell. During pregnancy I had relished mandarins. I looked down at the tiles in front of me. The last time I sat here, I was unable to see the floor, as my belly blocked my view. Ash lifted his head and gave a faint smile. I knew that this was hard for him too. To be honest, as the mother of our boys, I received an outpouring of support from everyone, but I wondered how Ash felt at this moment. He experienced the reality of the loss in a way that I was shielded from. He had witnessed the births of the triplets. He had seen me in pain as I reluctantly released those babies into the world. He had heard my cries of anguish; he had seen my stone face of shock and loss.

I reached over, gently stroked his arm, and smiled back at him encouragingly. The doctor called out my name, so Ash and I walked to the consultation room and took a seat. There were three other people in the room: the doctor who had spoken to us when I came into the hospital in labour, and two other women that I did not recognize. The doctor explained that one of the other ladies was a colleague of his and the third person was a student doctor. He asked for permission for her to stay. I did not mind. I just wanted to proceed with the meeting so that we could leave. The doctor explained that the triplets were born early because my uterus was unable to take the pressure of a first-time multiple pregnancy. He also mentioned that I was classed as subfertile, not infertile, as the only issue I had was irregular ovulation. He advised against us trying for multiples again but did not see any issue with a singleton pregnancy in the future. The doctor ended our conversation by commenting that my body had behaved perfectly normally under the circumstances. We left the appointment feeling relieved and slightly hopeful. The doctors and staff at the hospital could not have been more professional and caring, and we were grateful for the opportunity to have met with them. We walked out of the hospital hand in hand, ready to face the future together, whatever that would be.

Our Facebook post that mentioned donations to a small charity had an overwhelming response from our family and friends. To our absolute amazement, we found almost $15,000 had been donated. We marvelled at the generosity of people, and we could only imagine how many lives could be touched in South Africa with this money. Ash and I were honoured to be part of this miracle of kindness.

Wednesday, 19 March 2014

This morning an idea popped into my mind to write about our experience with losing our three babies. After reading each of my messages, I put my phone away and focused my attention on packing for our trip to South Africa.

I was desperate for a break from thinking about our loss, talking about our loss, and feeling those intense emotions when I remembered our experience. 'Weary' is the perfect word to describe my body, spirit, and soul. Like an unwanted jacket on a scorching hot day, the fabric of weariness stuck to my skin, reducing my comfort and restricting my movement. I wanted to be free, so I made up my mind to focus on the positive.

Monday, 24 March 2014

Diary Entry

> It's so good to be back in Cape Town. We love seeing our family and friends and just adore this diverse and interesting city. There is an atmosphere of possibility and hope. I am still trying to overcome jet lag, sitting up in bed at 5.00 a.m. We have plans to visit the safe house supported by Orphancare Foundation this morning.

Excited but nervous to see the babies in the safe homes, we stood at the gate and waited for the housemother to unlock it for us. Ash and I spent time in the school home of the safe house. We observed the lessons being taught and later discovered that this school home was actually one of the volunteer's bedrooms. She had given up her room so the children would have a place to learn. What a selfless act, giving up her comfort so these children could learn.

Ash and I played with the beautiful children and had fun with the songs and rhymes. Then they were led outside into the undercover play area after their morning tea snack. We were invited to visit with some of the new babies to the home. I braced myself and entered the nursery room. Captivated by the sweet tenderness of those precious children who had unfortunately been abandoned by their parents, we could not understand how anyone could leave these beautiful babies.

Carefully placing one arm underneath his tiny body, I held a newborn in the most comfortable position I could manage. His curly hair was propped up perfectly at the top of his head. I marvelled at his smooth, glossy skin. He smelled divine. I repositioned him closer and looked into his dark russet eyes. He was flawless. The soft fabric of his grow suit against my skin set off my tears. He was small and frail, but there was a sense of strength about this child. *He is a fighter,* I thought as I swayed him cautiously in my arms. Mesmerized by his eyes, I saw something striking, something vulnerable, and something precious.

What a journey it had been, but here I was, holding a miracle baby. The African-born beauty nestled close to my chest and brought emotions that were hard to fight.

Completely aware that I would have to hand him back in a few moments, I took in each detail of his gorgeous face and said a prayer over him. How fortunate he was to be totally sheltered from the truth of how we had been brought together in that moment. This little angel was none the wiser to the pain I had endured in recent months. This beautiful child rested peacefully in my arms. I hoped this was a prophetic picture of things to come.

Our visit to Cape Town was jam-packed with family visits, volunteering opportunities, shopping trips, and church events.

We were able to share the story of how God was healing us as we grieved the loss of our precious triplet boys. Each person we shared with was amazed at our resilience and peace about the whole situation. We explained that it was a process and some days were better than others, but also that we had an underlying assurance that God was bigger than this situation and we chose to look to Him to help us overcome the pain of this loss. We also declared that we had hope for a future with a child of our own.

Tuesday, 8 April 2014

Diary Entry

> Back in Australia! We are reinvigorated by all of the wonderful experiences in South Africa. I sense that God wants us to be hopeful about having children. I feel a peace about God's willingness for us to have a child.

As I enjoyed my cup of tea whilst sitting comfortably on our lounge room seat, I recorded the last few days' events in my journal as I reflected on all the conversations Ash and I had in Cape Town about losing the triplets. We found that there were a few common themes. Firstly, people were amazed at how well we were coping so soon after such a devastating loss. Secondly, they were encouraged by the story of the money donated from the other side of the world to a charity local to them. Thirdly, they reaffirmed our belief that we would have more children, as they spoke faith into our situation.

Thursday, 10 April 2014

Diary Entry

> I am having one of those dark days. I think I'm sad
> because I feel as though I've lost not only three precious
> boys but also dreams for their future. Why can't I shake
> these feelings? I have days when I don't think about our
> loss at all until I place my head on my pillow, but then
> there are days when I wake up and the thoughts attack
> like a bee sting, and all of a sudden the painful memories
> flood back. It takes me hours, sometimes even the whole
> day, to shake it off and to shift my focus away from those
> gloomy thoughts and dark feelings. God, I need your
> help. I can't do this on my own. Please help me!

I stared out the window at the beautiful view of pine trees and
grassland, all perfectly framed above the roses in our garden
across the balcony. Sadness about losing the boys rushed over me
again. This grieving process felt like one step forward, two steps
back, one step to the side, and one step forward again. Today I
was feeling particularly low. The sullen and grey clouds in the sky
reflected my mood in that moment.

At 1.17 a.m., I woke up and went to the bathroom. I started
thinking about seeing the gorgeous babies at our local church's
women's gathering. I was haunted by their well-formed, strong
bodies, rounded rosy cheeks and their happy mothers. All I could
do was cry. They were all perfectly healthy, but our boys never
made it that far.

As I sat sobbing, doubled over on the top of the closed toilet seat,
I wiped the tears from my eyes, cheeks, and chin with my sleeve.
Then, after a while, I closed my eyes and saw an image of myself
holding a baby in my arms. I knew it was my baby. This image
from God sent a flicker of hope to my heart. I acknowledged God's

goodness. I stopped crying, wiped my face once again, and then made my way back to bed.

I wrote in my journal using my phone light. It was the last page of this journal.

Diary Entry

> Having our own baby looks impossible right now, but I trust you, Lord!

Monday, 14 April 2014

We walked into the garage of our home for the first time in ages and saw all the baby equipment we had bought in anticipation of our babies. Ash and I talked about what to do with the baby furniture. We could keep one set and give the rest away to family or friends. *This is not how I expected things to be*, I told myself as I walked out behind Ash. When he had picked up each of those pieces of baby furniture months prior, I had not thought we would be giving them away or selling them before we had a chance to use them for our own children. Drawn into this roller coaster of emotions as we continued to grieve the loss of our boys, I decided to write the following positive reflection.

Diary Entry

> Life does not always turn out the way I expect, and yet I choose to hope on. I am starting to see our situation in a new light. My belief that our thoughts affect our emotions, and vice versa, is what pushes me ahead. I believe that emotions, like clouds, change; they come and go. Emotions are important, but they are also subject to my will. What I focus on will ultimately cause me to be either healthy or unhealthy in my thought life. I

have a choice and a part to play in how I react to my situation. Life can be horrible. Bad things happen. Death comes. Loss has to be faced throughout life. However, I have a choice to make. I don't deny the pain that comes when faced with loss, difficulty, unfairness, injustice, hurt, disappointments, abuse, mistreatments, misunderstanding, hatred, and prejudice, but I have the chance to choose how I will respond. I allow myself to experience the emotions in a safe and healthy way, and then, when I have had the release needed, I wipe my tears, wash my face, compose myself, and enter a peaceful, happy place in my thoughts. I refocus my attention on what is good. I don't allow myself to stay in the place of pain or mourning for longer than I need to. I focus on what is going right, what I do have, and how I can help others. I have fun on purpose. I allow healing to come through to me. My mind is powerful. If I choose to make good decisions with how I focus my attention, I am in a better place to move out of my pit of grief and regain my joy. I use my words to foster this new perspective, which gives me strength, and I challenge others who try to change my focus back to the pain. I read things that nourish my soul, I listen to things that nourish my soul, I watch things that nourish my soul, and I engage with people who nourish my soul. I choose to look forward. I choose to wipe the dust away, stand up, and then move ahead. I do this several times a day if needed, until it becomes my habit. It may take a long time to adopt this custom, but as I am dedicated to change, I commit myself to not giving up. I forgive myself when I fail this process or when I have a bad attitude about my situation. I think, speak, and act according to what I am hoping for, not according to what I see around me or what has happened in the past. I live congruently in this way. I help others who are struggling and funnel my time and energy not only to myself but also to those who are lonely, hurt, in need, or helpless. I try to show them how I have learned to cope and see them gain freedom from the pain and oppression of their situation. I choose to put myself in the place where others are and to help them in whatever way I can. I allow myself to have pyjama days when I just need a break from it all. I take one day at a time. I surround myself in a caring community. I choose not to isolate, no matter how much I feel like doing that. I learn from others. I laugh with others, and I cry with others.

Empowered by this new way of living, I decided to make a list of goals that I wanted to achieve in the next three months, in the following categories: physical, mental, emotional, spiritual, relational, vocational, and educational. It took me a few hours to articulate exactly what I wanted to achieve in each of these areas and to decipher ways in which I would be able to attain these goals. Working back from the goals, I planned the way I would spend my time on each of these areas.

Friday, 2 May 2014

Diary Entry

Got some news this morning that one of my friends is pregnant. For a moment, I gave in to self-pity, but I then willed myself to be happy for her. This baby is a gift from God, and I will celebrate! My will is stronger than my emotions.

This was one of those occasions when I needed to make a choice between wallowing in my own pain and disappointment or rejoicing with another person. I chose to be joyful. Children are a gift from God, and I celebrated with our friends and family members who were blessed in this way. Our experience would not sour me. Even though it was hard to face, I would face it head on. I reminded myself that I had strength to overcome this. I decided to text her congratulations and prayed for a healthy, safe pregnancy.

Friday, 9 May 2014

Crying at sporadic times during the day is something I was becoming accustomed to. Usually something triggered my memory and I began to feel an overwhelming sense of sadness. This happened when I least expected it. The tears usually left me feeling better. Reading *Good Grief* by Granger E. Westberg helped me to process my grief. Westberg says 'ultimately we can be healed of our bitterness and move ahead'. This is exactly what I am hoping for.

I read Matthew chapter 1, where there are names listed in the genealogy of Jesus (Matthew 1:1–17 NIV). I noticed four women's names. Each of these women faced life-changing situations and all kinds of losses. They each trusted God, and He saw them through. One could almost say that they came out better than before.

The story that stood out to me was that of Tamar. After losing her husband and then being cheated out of having children by her second husband, she was eventually blessed with twins. Each of these women—Tamar, Rahab, Ruth, and Mary—was faced with a choice of whether or not she would trust God or give in to the despair of her situation. It is not usually the easy option, but I was convinced that if we trust God, we will be better off.

Sunday, 11 May 2014

Diary Entry

It's Mother's Day. Today will test my resolve. God, please help me not to dwell on my loss but to celebrate mothers that have blessed my life.

Rather than becoming bitter because I was not celebrating with our three boys, I decided to do something special for my mother. I worked on a slideshow of all the photos I had stored away on my computer. We were hosting the Mother's Day dinner for our extended family, so I tidied the house, set up the lounge room and dining room, and prepared the food.

Ash wished me a happy Mother's Day and gave me a shiny blue stovetop kettle as a gift. I loved it from the moment I unwrapped it. We hugged as we stared out at the beautiful scenery through our lounge room window together. Immediately deciding to use my new gift, I picked it up on my way towards the doorway. Watching the kettle heat up on the stove, I daydreamed about receiving handmade paintings and unique Mother's Day stall presents, such as floral soaps, organic hand cream, and decadent chocolates. As a teacher, one of my favourite events in our school calendar was visiting the Mother's Day stalls with the younger children. I enjoyed planning craft activities for my students to make gifts to take home to their mothers. Mid-thought, I became painfully aware that this would not be something that I would experience for many years. The tears welled up again.

Missing out on motherhood was only one area of my life that I longed to see change. Many parts of my life were bringing me fulfilment: marriage, family relationships, and friendships, to name a few. I had travelled to numerous places around the world, gained experiences, and learned from different cultures. The pleasure of singing my own songs for people in other countries, and meeting unique and accommodating people from all walks of life, was already part of my journey so far. I thought myself happy and drank my tea with a smile. Life was hard, but there was always light and shade. If I focused on the shade for too long, I would be lost and depressed, but if I looked for the light, the silver linings around the dark clouds of my life, I was sure to discover hope again. *Should I prepare myself with the correct mindset, clothing, and umbrella and face the relentless rain or emotional storm with courage, or should I run and hide away in a dark and lonely place?* This was a daily choice. In fact, it was a choice I had to make every few hours, and sometimes every few minutes. *How would I look back on these days? Would I be happy with my response? Would I see resilience and tenacity in my behaviour? Would my words be filled with hope or helplessness and doubt?*

Since losing the triplets, I had noticed a change in myself—a kind of strengthening. It was a transformation in the way I was responding not only to our loss but also to how I viewed myself. Pain and abuse had wounded me in the past, and I had experienced incredible healing, but now a new adversity had threatened to steal my joy again. I believed that I was being refined by the fire of this situation, shaped by the pain of this grief, and strengthened by the weakening of this disappointment. My reality was ruled by a different set of principles because I believed in the unseen world. This world exchanged joy for mourning and hope for despair. It replaced beauty for ashes and offered confidence in the future. It promised eternal life. A loving God governed this unseen world I had signed up for, and if I chose truth over what I perceived through my broken lens of pain, I would receive His reward. I reminded myself that He was near to me when others weren't able to be. He was closer than any earthly or spiritual force. He held the universe in place, and He would always be my Lord.

A documentary about Beyoncé Knowles's life depicts a time in her life when she unfortunately experienced the loss of a child. A talented and driven woman, she showed great vulnerability in sharing her story in this short film. It amazes me how losing babies affects so many people in the world. I did not believe that this was the natural order of things, and yet it happens so often. Some statistics suggest that 25 per cent of all women who become pregnant end up having a miscarriage. That is about one in four pregnancies. Since the deaths of our boys, I have had many conversations with women about their own tragedies of losing children. Some healed through the years, while others are still longing for that child that did not survive. Some mothers struggled through the pain on their own. Some mothers had a secret birthday celebration, however unhappy the occasion was, in remembrance of the absent baby.

Grieving well was important to me. I chose to cooperate with God so my heart would be whole again. There would be scars and sad memories of this tragedy, but I wanted to be able to speak about Summer, Snow, and Sky with hope. People would leave a conversation with me believing that whatever they were facing, whatever they were mourning over, the promise was that joy would come in the morning. 'Weeping may stay overnight, but there is joy in the morning' (Psalm 30:5 CSB).

For me, discovering the path of healing came in many different forms, including connecting with others who were in need. Shifting the focus away from myself, even momentarily, brought peace. I encouraged myself by believing that one day my children would run around in our backyard, laughing happily. I swallowed down the pain that this longing brought to the surface, and I kept my mind on the possibility of 'one day'. One day I would hear my children call out, 'Mum,' and I would laugh out loud.

Sunday, 25 May 2014

<u>Diary Entry</u>

> I met with a friend and talked about the possibilities of 2015. As I was writing in my journal, this thought popped into my head: 'Focus on South Africa'. Then I

spent about an hour looking at children's homes in South Africa.

After completing my diary entry, I was intrigued about that last instruction about South Africa, so I looked up information about helping young women in that country. In my research, I discovered a directory of all the groups helping young women and children on their national government website. Reading through the information gave me a sense of confidence that at some point in the future I would be helping some of these girls.

Staring out the window of my parked car, I noticed a lady carrying a small baby swaddled in a pink wrap. She adjusted the child's body in her arms. The mother looked tired. No tears flooded my eyes this time. I just smiled and continued texting my friend.

Thursday, 29 May 2014

Diary Entry

> I had a few intense moments with Ash. He said some wise words this morning about my attitude. He suggested that my attitude is bordering on envy. I really need to focus on being content. Why do I get so worked up about little things that don't matter? Why do I criticize so easily? Why am I so frustrated that those who have what I want see it as a burden, when I would see it as my greatest honour? God, please help me to see the good in all people and to think the best of everyone. God, please forgive me for my proud and selfish attitude.

Most of the time, I did not want what other people had. I was usually happy with what I had in my life; but since we lost the triplets, I had begun resenting people who enjoyed successful pregnancies. I realized that this was unfair to all parents, whose only crime was being fortunate enough to have healthy children. *'What's wrong with me, God?'* I asked this question several times a day. I struggled with doubting that God loved me as much as He loved them, because I had been left with the empty cot. In my head, I knew this was all nonsense, but my heart was telling a different story. I longed to be a mother. I longed to hold a baby of our own in my arms.

Wiping away the tears, I reached down to the coffee table for a tissue. *Was this ever going to end?* I tried to compose myself. I had cried many tears over the past few months. I knew that God had a purpose for this pain, but I struggled to see what it could be. I convinced myself that focusing on a project, other people, or a future dream might be the very thing to lift me out of this emotional crater.

The resting place of the triplets.

4

WEARY WINTER

Tuesday, 3 June 2014

After my counselling placement session, I was exhausted, but my heart was full. I was thoroughly enjoying my work at the aged care facility. The staff and residents were friendly and welcoming, and I had already begun a friendship with one of the other psychology students. I was fascinated by the lives represented in this restful facility. Some of the people had lived through the Second World War. There were accounts of hiding from the bombs, sad stories of losing loved ones, and dramatic tales of escape across country borders. The common themes with these narratives were that the storytellers were close to their communities, hard working, and sacrificed a lot to survive. Everyone pulled together through the tough times, and nobody wasted or took anything for granted. How I relished listening to their experiences. My role as the counsellor was to listen, empathize, and allow them to enjoy sharing their tales. These sessions inspired and humbled me as I realized what the past generations had endured so I could live in a country that offered me so much.

Our own migration story from South Africa to Australia had its heroes. My great-aunt and great-uncle made the difficult decision to leave South Africa to travel to an unknown land in search of a better future for their children. Not long after, my grandparents and their children followed, making it possible for us to join them. If it weren't for these courageous individuals, my life would look very different. I will always be eternally grateful for the sacrifices and forethought of my relatives.

Thursday, 17 June 2014

Diary Entry

I had a little cry this morning as I thought about the fact that this is the week that our boys were due to be born, according to our original ultrasound scan. For a moment, I started to think about how life would have been if all had gone to plan with our triplets, but this just made me upset.

The anniversaries of various events in the lives and deaths of our triplet boys left me feeling hollow. It was a conscious choice to focus on the positives and strengths in my life to avoid spiralling down into a depressive state.

A few days later, closing my left eye to correct the eyeliner that was running along my top eyelid, I grunted as the car lurched forward. I sighed as I turned to look at Ash with my crooked eyeliner in place. He apologized. Silence filled the air and I instantly realized that it was unfair of me to project my frustration onto him. If I were more organized, I would not need to do my make up in the car on the way to church. Feeling the guilt hover over me, I quickly apologized and put my cosmetic instruments of torture away.

Today had been a difficult day. I was struggling to keep my thoughts moving in a positive direction, and my frustration and unpleasant emotions were unrelenting. Keeping my tongue securely in my mouth cavity during those moments of annoyance was my only hope of making it through without taking out victims with my lacerating tongue. I fought the urge to express how exasperated I was feeling, as I knew this wouldn't help either of us.

We walked into the church building and were greeted by an entourage of friendly faces. By the time I reached my seat, I was already in a better mood. Some days it was harder to shift my damp emotions, but today I was on top of it. The singers, musicians, and hosting staff created a comfortable environment, and I eased into singing the familiar songs. The message spoken was one of encouragement, and I sensed strength infusing into my soul as I walked out of the building.

As Ash and I moved out to the foyer, a close friend stopped us and handed us one large gift bag, one small gift bag, and a card. Confused but delighted, I opened the beautifully wrapped objects to find a picture of a snow scene with the sun streaming across a blue-and-purple sky. The words 'Summer, Snow, and Sky' were printed on the top of this picturesque landscape. Seeing the names of our triplet boys illustrated in such a stunning picture brought a lump to my throat, and tears began to trickle out. I looked in the gift box and discovered a delicate heart-shaped necklace with the letter S inscribed on the front. Ash opened his box and saw an equally beautiful key ring marked with a gold letter S. With my emotions rushing to the surface, I did not make any attempt to hide how I was feeling but took a moment to thank our friends for this thoughtful, generous gift. They explained that the necklace and key ring were gifts from the leaders of our church, given to let us know that we were loved. Overwhelmed by this kindness, Ash and I walked out of our church with hearts full of gratitude.

Once in our car, I allowed myself to feel those emotions without reserve. It was a sombre drive home, but I was encouraged that there were such thoughtful and loving people not in the world out there but in my own personal world.

Saturday, 5 July 2014

<u>Diary Entry</u>

> We have an appointment with our fertility specialist today. Feeling numb, I would rather postpone this meeting, but I know that when I shrink back from difficult situations, I regret it later. So here goes ...

As Ash stopped the car in a park outside of the fertility specialist's clinic, I adjusted my coat and took a quick look in the visor mirror. This was the first time we had seen our doctor since we lost our triplets, and the trepidation of the situation was playing with my state of peace.

Ash took my hand as we climbed the narrow set of stairs to the consulting rooms. The last time we were at this place, I was filled with hope. This time things were different. Like a freight train approaching high speed, my heart pounded as I tried to catch my breath. I swallowed quietly, took my seat in the waiting room, and tried to calm myself down. None of the magazines on the corner coffee table looked appealing, so I took my phone out of my bag and tried to distract myself by checking emails, social media accounts—anything to keep my mind off what I was about to face.

Occasionally I looked up at Ash, who was also looking at his phone. He sensed me staring at him and smiled encouragingly. Desperately trying to control the negative thoughts in my head and the butterflies in my stomach, I shifted position a few times.

I moved my bag from one side of my seat to the other, pulled at the front of my top, and even removed some lint from the sleeve of my cardigan, but nothing seemed to help. I could not ignore that sinking feeling that this, too, would come to naught.

The doctor entered the waiting room and said my name as she adjusted the folder in her hands. We both looked up from our phones, and I smiled up at her. Ash and I followed her into her consulting suite, and I tried to remember to breathe. The mood in the room was unnerving as our doctor worked hard not to upset us. She carefully discussed our case and future procedures. Grateful for her kind and attentive manner, I imagined this meeting must have been very difficult for her. The appointment was brief but encouraging, and we headed out of the clinic relieved and hopeful.

Monday, 4 August 2014

Diary Entry

> I thought that I was okay with this ovulation induction procedure but had a total meltdown with Ash that went on for nearly an hour. He is so wise, as he kept on reminding me that God is good. God's ways are higher than ours, and His thoughts are higher than ours. I know this to be true and was reminded by God just a few days ago of the part in the Bible this verse comes from. I've come to the conclusion that God is developing faithfulness in me. I find it very easy to give up on things, but God wants me to stick to the plans that He has given us. As I was driving, God showed me a series of pictures in my mind's eye which illustrated times when I was desperate to see immediate results. Rather than waiting patiently, I gave up, quit, or moved on and lost the opportunity to receive the good results. This was a helpful reminder. Thank you, God.

Choosing to spoil myself, I bought new pyjamas as I chatted away with my mother about her health. She had been going for walks around her neighbourhood block and said that it helped her to feel better. We stopped for a coffee at our favourite cafe and chatted about how the rest of our family members were doing and how I was coping with the loss of our triplets. My mother had recently been babysitting my three nieces, and she relayed some treasured conversations and moments of her time with them.

A wave of sadness hit me as I realized that my mother would not be able to babysit our triplets. She had been excited to meet them and welcome them into our family, and it was clear that she had also felt the loss very deeply. Our faith in God was what helped us, and we turned our conversation to focus on the truth of God's eternal plan and how there were certain things in life that we would never understand. We had both experienced God's unfailing love and kindness in our lives, which spurred us on to believe that this was not the end of our story.

As I drove home that afternoon, I thought back to a conversation I had with a church leader after we shared the news of losing our boys. I distinctly remember him saying, 'This is not the end of your story.' He had a glow in his eyes, and I could see that he believed every word of that statement. At the time I agreed, mostly out of politeness, as I desperately wanted to have the same level of faith as he did for our future, but my mind was filled with thoughts of doubt. Although at that time I believed that God faithfully healed us and brought us through the grief and loss of our boys, I was struggling to believe that He was going to do anything more in this area of our lives.

Our experience of loss could be described as arriving back from a harrowing journey through a wilderness or a jungle with nothing but the clothes on our backs. I'd told my tale of escape from the clutches of death and still bore the scars of the ordeal, but to believe that I could go through another one of those experiences and survive felt overly optimistic. I was not looking forward to facing any new adventures or trials in the near future. My dilemma was that Ash and I had agreed to try again, spurred on by a prompting and several encouragements from God.

Sitting in the waiting room of the fertility clinic, I tried to remain positive. There was an odd sense of hope and possibility mixed with a tinge of anxiety in my heart. I watched as women of all ages walked in and out of the clinic. I noticed women in heels, runners, sandals, and other casual shoes as I kept my eyes focused on the carpet in front of me. Looking down at my own shoes, I realized that I was just one amongst thousands seeking to become a mother. My emotions betrayed me as tears began to well in my eyes, and I raced out to the toilet to avoid being caught crying. A kind receptionist glanced at me as I passed her on my way down the corridor and towards the toilet sign. Sitting in the cubicle, I closed my eyes and let the tears flow freely. I was grateful that I ran out of time to put makeup on that morning before the appointment. Sniffling quietly, I pulled the tissues out of my bag and dabbed the tears streaming down my cheeks. Other patrons came and went as I sat and allowed myself to weep. It took me a few minutes to compose myself, but I made the decision to face this process with courage. I did not know how this cycle would end. I hoped we would conceive and I would be able to hold my child in my arms. Maybe I would be granted the chance to watch our child grow, but if that was not my story, I would still believe that God loved me and that He was faithful. In moments like those, I was grateful for the voices of positivity in my life. I drew strength from what was spoken over me and to me. Uplifting words from the past helped when I was overwhelmed with emotion, especially when I was perched on the toilet seat in the public toilet of a fertility clinic. I thanked God for His patience, asked Him to help me remain courageous, and then washed face and my hands and headed back to the waiting room.

Diary Entry

> I am looking out our lounge room window at the dark clouds that are moving across from right to left. The clouds appear dark and heavy, filled with the promise of rain, but they are moving, and they are not stopping. These clouds are passing, not staying. The dark patches of life are the same. They are not here to stay forever, but only for a while.

After writing this in my diary, I took one more look up at the sky and was surprised to see that the clouds I was staring at, the very ones that inspired these previous reflections, were now a lighter grey. There was rain in the distance, but I could still see through the rain.

The fertility clinic called to tell me that our last cycle had been unsuccessful. In order to avoid multiple conceptions, we had been using much less of the FSH. It came as no surprise to me that this cycle had not worked. After sitting with the disappointment for a while, I clearly heard God say, 'Don't give up.'

I hoped that these clouds would not stay forever.

Diary Entry

> My life looks different to the way I expected it to turn out, but I trust God for my next move. As I closed my eyes in meditation, I heard a gentle whisper: 'In quietness and trust will be your strength' (Isaiah 30:15 NIV). I'm not in charge or in control of what happens to me, but I can choose my response.

A friend of mine asked me how I was able to cope with this loss so well. I confided that I had my moments of sadness, disappointment, hopelessness, doubt, and frustration. Of course, I knew that God was the one who was healing my heart. He was the one who made this awful loss less traumatic and gave me hope for the future. He was the one who believed in me and comforted me. He was the one who gave me the strength I needed when I faced tough situations, such as seeing healthy newborn babies. He was the one who promised me that good days were ahead. There was much more that I could say about God's role in my life, especially during this dark season. To be completely honest, my healing came from a combination of sources initiated by God.

My connection with God, which was first and foremost the key to my restoration, brought me hope at every moment. Then my relationships with my family and friends brought relief as I talked about our loss and as they prayed for me. Engaging in helping others alleviated my own difficulties and it was a welcome change for my heart and mind to focus on someone else's journey. Physical exercise played its role in helping my body to recover quickly and released wonderful hormones that lifted me and made me feel good. I trained my thoughts to remain moving in a positive direction by meditating on the promises that God had given me as His daughter. I remembered to speak in this way when I discussed our loss and recovery. Also, though I failed many, many times, I tried to remember to be kind and patient with myself. Lastly, working on other projects proved helpful in rebuilding my confidence and keeping my focus securely on the possibilities that lay in the future.

I believed God worked in and through each of these areas to restore my spirit, soul, and body.

Sunday, 10 August 2014

<u>Diary Entry</u>

> We made the long-awaited trip to Portsea today.
> Another step in our healing has brought up those
> painful memories, and I'm struggling to keep my mind
> orientated in a positive direction. God, please help us!
> Help us to heal completely.

Ash parked the car, and I opened the window, looking at the clouds above. It was a sunny day, but the wind kept the chill alive just enough for me to be glad that I had packed my winter jacket. Tightness in my stomach and my sweaty palms revealed the restlessness I was feeling about this day. Ash and I had hardly said a word to each other as we drove to this special place.

With worship music still playing on the car stereo, I tried not to get caught up in the words, which could easily set me off into a blubbering mess. It had taken us six months to be ready for this event, and I was not going to sabotage any of it by getting caught up in fear.

I was in no rush to move out of the car as we sat staring out the windscreen. In our own ways, I believed that we were summoning our inner strength to do what needed to be done. We discussed today's event and agreed that this was the next step in our path of healing. I smoothed my fingers over the S pendant of the necklace I had been gifted by our church and said a silent prayer.

Grabbing my jacket from the backseat, I glanced at the box in the bag from the funeral service home and then turned to face the front of the car, fighting the temptation to cry. Stepping onto the beach, I let the breeze rush over me, taking in its cool, energizing breath.

Ash clasped my hand, and we walked along the sand together. The last time our feet touched this beach was a day that changed our lives forever. That was a significant day, because it was the day I became Ash's fiancé. The memory of that happy time, marked by its exuberance and hope, contrasted with today's sombre occasion. We had chosen this place because it meant a lot to us.

With the wind blowing my curls across my face, I tried to shake off the overwhelming sorrow I felt growing with each step. Memories flashed in my mind of the aftermath of labour and the ache I felt in hospital bed. The fight to stay the course and bring their ashes to a final resting place was beginning to ask more of me than I thought I had inside. Ash held on to my hand and kept stepping towards the large rock formation in the water. We had climbed this rock on the day of our engagement. We had stood on the edge of this rock as Ash asked the question that my heart longed to hear. It was on this rock that we hugged as future husband and wife. And now it was on this rock that we would lay our boys to rest forever.

Fortunately the beach was deserted and we could take comfort that we could do this important ceremony in private. We stopped regularly to take photos, as we wanted this day to remain part of our lives. Ash and I approached the rock formation and stood mesmerized by the waves washing into the cavern, which had been formed by the water over many years. I pressed play on my phone, and we listened to 'Oceans' by Hillsong United. We stood and allowed our tears to flow as we watched the foam of the waves swirl over the rocks below. The song became a soundtrack to the calming rhythm of the water gushing in and out of this watery crypt.

We asked God for strength and released the remains of our little boys into the ocean. The water took their ashes out through the crevices of the rocks and further than we could see. Sobbing intensely, I felt the pain in my heart dissolve. Wiping the salty tears across my cheek, I whispered, 'I trust you, Lord.'

Hollow but hopeful, we stood and allowed the movement of the waves to comfort us, and we held on to each other, listening to the music and allowing our spirits to experience each hopeful note and lyric.

I heard voices behind us and assumed that there were others eager to savour the tranquillity of this beautiful place. After a few moments, I motioned to Ash that we should leave; but when I looked around, I could not see anyone. Confused by the absence of the people I had just heard talking about us, only a few steps behind, I looked at Ash and asked, 'Where are the people?'

'What people?' he replied, looking back and forth.

'The ones I heard talking,' I replied, looking back up the beach in both directions.

'There wasn't anyone here,' Ash said, finally climbing off the rock.

'Yes they were …' My voice trailed off as I noticed that there were only two sets of footprints along the beach leading towards where we stood.

I asked God whom I had heard behind us. He answered, 'They were angels. I sent them to help you say goodbye.'

Astonished at the meaning of what I heard God say, I just looked up and froze for a few moments. I felt God speak those words into my spirit, and it became clear that the living God cared deeply for us.

Thursday, 28 August 2014

<u>Diary Entry</u>

> Last night I had a strange dream about being in heaven. I saw my dad (who passed away years ago) playing an unfamiliar instrument. He was happy to see me. As soon as I saw him, I knew that I was in heaven. He seemed relaxed and filled with joy. As I looked through a doorway to the right, I could see three little boys. These were the same boys from the vision I had back in February. All three of them looked similar but not identical. Each had a musical instrument in his hands. I had a strong sense that these were our boys—Summer, Snow, and Sky. My father instructed them to play together, and as soon as I heard them play a beautiful harmony, I woke up.

Jolted awake by the dream, I tried to hold on to each detail. It was one of those vivid dreams that felt real. After the initial reflection of what I had just experienced, I began to cry. I missed my boys, but the dream was a gift. I knew that their spirits lived on in heaven with my father, my grandparents, and all the others who have gone before us into our eternal resting place.

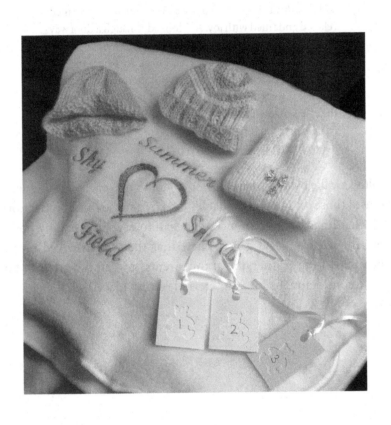

5

STRUGGLING IN SPRING

Sunday, 7 September 2014

<u>Diary Entry</u>

As I meditated this morning, I had a clear picture. I was sitting before a throne in a palace. Desperate for God to hear my cry for a child, I knelt face down. I saw the word 'October', and then the vision disappeared. I'm not sure what this means, but I believe that October is a significant month.

Wednesday, 1 October 2014

<u>Diary Entry</u>

I can't believe that we are in October already. Over a year ago, I found out that I was pregnant with our three boys.

Standing in the reception room at a friend's wedding, I struggled to be positive about our loss. People I had not seen for years made comments about the triplets and the posts they had seen on social media. I was not enthused to discuss it, even though

I knew that they were trying to be supportive and encouraging. That evening, I hid behind my extroverted personality. I tried but failed miserably to contain my emotions, replacing them with irritatingly obnoxious behaviour.

In bed the next morning, after several snoozed alarms, I relived my unpleasant behaviour at the wedding. Disappointed at myself, I stepped into the shower and tried to wash it all away. There was something very soothing about showers. I was not sure whether this was because I enjoyed solitude or because I often heard God's voice speaking to me when I was showering. God's voice featured in many different places and spaces of my life; I did not hear it only in a church or when I prayed.

Long walks and lonely paths were ideal for engaging my spirit in hearing from God. For me, there was a heightened awareness of God's presence when I was out in nature. God spoke to me when I sat and meditated on the truth of the Bible. However, hearing Him speak was not limited to one place or one way. My relationship with God meant that He often whispered ideas, showed me pictures and visions, and prompted me to pray for people throughout my day, even when I was doing the dishes! I would also clearly detect His voice when I was with people in our faith community or with close family or friends. It appeared to be easier when we met together with the same focus in mind, but it could also happen at parties and other social events.

The key for me to hear Him speak was having an open and humble heart. I was by no means walking around with a halo on my head. In the same way a gardener keeps his or her garden tidy, healthy, and neat by weeding regularly, I needed God's help to weed out the things that were harmful and unhealthy. If I maintained a 'weedless heart' by bringing those things to Him that were unhelpful, I often heard Him speak with clarity.

Thursday, 2 October 2014

Diary Entry

> Today I felt a little sorry for myself when I heard about how other people are doing exciting and adventurous things. I had a short pity party and then came to my senses. I cheered myself up by planning the girls' night for this Sunday.

Not exempt from being self-focused, some days I struggled to keep my attention orientated in a healthy direction. Jealousy and envy are not attractive or desirable traits, but they are certainly ones that I took on from time to time. Social connection often bumped me off those tracks of thinking, and I was grateful for my village of beautiful, strong, and amazing family and friends who helped me overcome this character flaw.

Thursday, 9 October 2014

Diary Entry

I spoke to the nurse at the fertility clinic, and she said that I should start injecting the stimulating hormones. She also booked a blood test for me on Monday. Since the negative results of our last cycle, I have decided to have a good attitude through this process, even if it is unsuccessful.

Saturday, 11 October 2014

Diary Entry

> My nephew was born today. I am happy for my brother-in-law, sister-in-law, and their family, but I am still

struggling. My upset may also be the result of having hormone injections. So far I have had four injections since Wednesday night. I am booked in for a blood test tomorrow, so the medical team at the fertility clinic will determine what needs to happen next. I had another mini meltdown yesterday. These hormone injections are making me edgy and highly sensitive.

Notebook in hand, I counted how many days it may be before I found out if I was pregnant, provided this cycle was successful. I found pleasure in planning ahead in hope. However, if things didn't turn out the way I expected, this habit created torment rather than pleasure. The medical procedures were gifts to couples unable to conceive, and I was grateful that we were in the position to benefit from medical science and technology in this way, but there were definite side effects, which resulted in me being physically and emotionally drained.

My all-day lecture seemed to take every ounce of my strength, and I was grateful when the lecturer announced that we would end a little earlier than normal. I thoroughly enjoyed her sessions, but today was particularly tough because of an encounter at the end of the session. Someone in class made a comment about me having children and confused me for another student who was a mother of three. Ordinarily this harmless mistake would have no effect on me. However, today was different. Overwhelmingly sad, I felt the current of tears rising as I left the building. It was dark out in the street, so wearing sunglasses would not work. Fortunately, because it was dark outside, no one could see my tears or my red, flushed face. I commanded myself to cry the hot tears out. I sobbed all the way to the train station but then composed myself, as the lights in the station were likely to give me away.

Of course, I had no hard feelings towards that forgetful classmate. She obviously had no idea of the impact of her words on my sensitive, wounded heart, but nonetheless it was still a difficult situation for me.

Visiting our newborn nephew was challenging mostly because he was related to us; he was one of our clan. Our relatives were very kind, and we were able to put our own feelings aside for a few moments to celebrate their beautiful baby. We had a pleasant visit and then headed home. Resting my head on my pillow after this hectic day gave me a sense of joy as I realized that I was much further along in my grieving process than I thought. If I had faced a day like this a few months before, or even a few weeks before, I likely would not have coped as well.

Saturday, 18 October 2014

Diary Entry

> I had another scan at the clinic this morning. We are very close to trying to get pregnant again. This procedure has taken longer than before, as our specialist is trying to be extra careful.

Ash and I walked back to our car along the Yarra River from the restaurant that hosted my high school reunion. I recounted my experience of reconnecting with several of my old friends. It was a great night of reminiscing about our school days, camps, excursions, plays, performances, and eccentric staff and students. Many of my classmates at the reunion had heard about the loss of our triplets and showed kindness and compassion as I shared parts of our story. The cold truth was that everyone had faced some kind of loss, difficulty, or struggle in life. The comforting reality was that even though our stories were different, by sharing them with each other we could connect in a deep and personal way as we absorbed strength from each other.

Monday, 20 October 2014

Diary Entry

> I've had several blood tests and ultrasound scans and found out that my pregnancy hormone levels are very low, which probably means that I am not pregnant. Again I found courage by reading the Bible and reminding myself that God is powerful and hasn't forgotten me. The process of trying to have children is just a process. *I am not a victim* of this situation. I currently have an illness that makes it difficult to become pregnant naturally.
>
> God whispered, 'Don't give up' this morning. So I won't give up! This is just one aspect of my life that is hard at the moment. There are plenty of areas that are easy, enjoyable, and rewarding. I will keep my chin up. I will look forward to celebrating the day that our child is born. I will trust God in this!

My will was stronger than my emotions and more enduring than any situation. I decided that I would use my time wisely, use my gifts and talents to help others, keep my eyes focused on the important things, be grateful for my wonderful life, use what was in my hands, be positive even when things around me were negative, and rely on God's wisdom for my life.

I spoke to Ash about our cycle not being successful, and we agreed that this would not stop us. The power of agreement is unshakeable. God told us not to give up, so we decided we would not. Things might not happen according to our timing, but we are not God, so that's okay. His timing is perfect.

Excited and energized by our declaration not to give up on having children, Ash and I discussed our plans for the following year. We both felt a pull towards spending two months in South

Africa. We ate our dinner and dreamed of the possibilities for our trip. We would love to volunteer our time to help orphaned and vulnerable children.

Thursday, 13 November 2014

<u>Diary Entry</u>

Today during my time of prayer and worship, I saw an image of a sunrise. I sensed that this symbol was God's way of telling me that a new day is dawning. This season is about to end, and a new season is about to begin.

Monday, 24 November 2014

<u>Diary Entry</u>

I woke up at 8.00 a.m. and went for a blood test at the fertility clinic. My veins are tired of all these tests. I have bruise marks and broken skin all up my arms. This doesn't seem right. Why is it taking so long? I am frustrated with the many trips to the clinic, and although the nurses and doctors are extremely kind and helpful, I just want this whole procedure to be over. I know that I am not being very grateful right now, but I am tired and drained. I don't feel like continuing, but I will honour this commitment to complete this cycle.

Thursday, 27 November 2014

<u>Diary Entry</u>

I have been going into the clinic for blood tests or scans several times a week. I know that taking the medication in smaller doses requires a lot of checking and patience, but it feels as if my patience barrel is empty. God, please give me strength.

As I walked out of the clinic, I readjusted my bag and checked that my phone and keys were still there. I took my usual walk down the main road where the clinic was situated and dashed across the road carefully. This ideal parking spot enabled me to park without a fee or the frustration of having to wait a long time for someone to leave the busy clinic. Once back in my car, I put on my seatbelt and suddenly had a sinking feeling. Looking in my side mirror, I murmured to myself as I waited for the last car to pass me before I could enter the main road. Frustrated at the routine of these appointments coupled with the fear that every ounce of effort was coming to nothing, I felt lower than I had for a while. I began to soak in those self-pitying emotions.

Stopped at the traffic lights further up the road, I glanced across to my left. My eye caught the passenger of the car next to me. This person was wearing a beanie, even though it was a warm day. I concluded by observing the person closely that this individual was a cancer patient. Shocked and moved to sadness, I smiled at that beautiful face and stared solemnly into those eyes, which were marked with pain. She did not smile back but stared blankly at me, with a slight curiosity crossing her brow. The traffic lights changed, and the car that housed that beautiful but tortured body moved forward and out of my sight. Woken from my dazed state by the horn of the car behind me, I jumped into motion and drove my car forward. The impact of what I had just witnessed hit my heart like an arrow. I instantly apologized to God for my stinking attitude as my throat became tight with emotion and tears formed in my eyes. I swallowed hard and decided to end my own pity party.

As I drove home, I reflected on the fact that there were many people suffering in far greater circumstances with worse prognoses than mine. This sober train of thought reminded me that I had committed to being grateful for everyone and everything in my life. I mentally made a list of the top ten things I could celebrate right there in the car.

I knew I was learning to be grateful. I was learning to be patient. Those two qualities could be achieved only by being made to wait for something that I longed for—something I desired, something outside of my control—and by being grateful for what was going right.

God had been so good to me, so I decided that the best thing to do at that moment was sing. I lifted my voice to my faithful, loving God as I sang praise songs loudly in my car all the way home. With each song, I felt light, hopeful, and at peace.

6

SUMMER STORIES

Saturday, 6 December 2014

<u>Diary Entry</u>

> Today is the last class of my counselling course! I cannot believe that I have finally finished. As much as this course was about me learning how to help others, I feel as though I have experienced healing, clarity, and growth. I'm so thankful for the lecturers and for the connections made with my fellow students.

We all applauded as our lecturer ended the session. A few of my classmates and I stayed around after class, marvelling at the fact that this was our last ever class for this course. We discussed our plans, and I explained that Ash and I were going to South Africa for two months. As the words flowed out of my mouth, I instantly felt at peace with this decision. I was surprised at my own enthusiasm and about using my counselling skills to make a difference in the lives of others.

Sunday, 7 December 2014

<u>Diary Entry</u>

> I am feeling nervous about what we have been asked to
> do this afternoon, but I know that this may help someone
> who is stuck in grief, so I will choose to face this day with
> boldness.

Stepping onto the stage at the Athenaeum Theatre with the
rest of the panel members at the evening church service was an
experience that I would never forget. Ash and I were asked to
share our story of the loss of our triplets and how God helped us
to heal. Anyone who knows me will confidently attest to the fact
that I enjoy sharing my life stories. In this case, however, I was
concerned about the subsequent conversations and how people
would treat us after they knew our struggles.

As we huddled backstage, I wished with all my heart that Ash
would get out of his shift at work and join me for both of the
services. I tried not to show how nervous I was, but I smiled
politely at everyone, including the stage manager and the worship
team members. Our pastor introduced everyone, and we took our
place at the beautifully decorated table. I braced myself for what
was to come. Each person at the table shared his or her story and
highlighted what God had done to help him or her through his
or her ordeals.

All I could do was pray that I did not start to cry while telling my
story. The time had come for me to share, and I looked across the
table at the pastor and all of the panel members staring back at me.
I lifted the microphone towards my mouth and took a deep breath.
I knew that God had used this story to bring healing and hope
to many people already, so I drew in every ounce of courage and
openly talked about our loss and how God had showed Himself

faithful. I spoke of the dark moment that I cried out to Him in our bedroom and how He graciously encouraged me, healed me, and restored my faith.

After the service, many people came up to me to thank me for sharing my story and for being so open and vulnerable. There were people with tears in their eyes, some of whom seemed genuinely moved by the words that I shared, and people who told me that they would take my words of courage into their own difficult situations.

Overjoyed at the impact of what sharing our story had already done, I was excited to share it again. Having Ash on stage with me brought an extra element of comfort, and this time the story seemed to flow better. I was less hesitant and talked with confidence. A family in the congregation who had suddenly lost several relatives in the past year took great courage from what we shared and came to the realization that they needed God to heal their wounded hearts. Gratitude filled my heart as I once again realized the truly miraculous work God had done in our lives. The story of Summer, Snow, and Sky has thrust us into people's love and affection—yet another blessing from their short, precious lives.

Wednesday, 10 December 2014

Diary Entry

> Went to the fertility clinic for a blood test. I am feeling the side effects of the medication. In 2005, a minister told me that I would be a 'Mother of many'. I am trying to hold on to that promise today.

Ash helped me mix some of the medication together and then had to leave while I injected it. I was shocked at Ash's obvious discomfort when I took out the needle to inject the medication. He said that he was sorry that I had to do this, but I tried to relieve his concern by telling him that I was used to needles and all kinds of intrusive procedures, as I had experienced both many times in recent months. I don't think this admission brought him much comfort, and I instantly regretted my frankness. I urged him to leave the room, as it seemed like the kind thing to do.

Friday, 12 December 2014

Diary Entry

> I was miserable yesterday and am feeling miserable today. I'm exhausted from fighting for everything. I went for another blood test. This feels like a waste of time, energy, money, petrol, and all this effort. I know my attitude stinks today, but I just don't care.

During times like these, I knew that the best thing to do was to shift my focus to helping someone else. I decided to rejoin the volunteer welcome team at our church. The leader was happy for me to step in straight away. I already felt better about keeping my thoughts on someone other than myself.

Wednesday, 17 December 2014

Diary Entry

> I started spotting this morning. Clearly this cycle was unsuccessful and I am not pregnant. Ash seemed very sad, but he said he still believes that God will give us children. I was expecting myself to be incredibly upset, but I'm actually okay. Even with this disappointing news, I still believe that this is going to be a good Christmas.

Friday, 19 December 2014

<u>Diary Entry</u>

I took a pregnancy test. The results were negative, as we expected. Of course, I am disappointed that I am not pregnant. I'm focused on Christmas and what God has planned for us for 2015. To be honest, I feel relieved that we can take a break from all the procedures, tests, appointments, and ultrasound scans and talk about how my hormones are doing. We haven't given up on having kids; we're just going to have a rest for a while.

Friday, 26 December 2014

<u>Diary Entry</u>

Ash and I had a terrific holiday with friends. We arrived home on Christmas Eve and thoroughly enjoyed our Christmas celebrations, just as I hoped we would! As I was waiting quietly during my time with God, images of Ash and me with a child flashed in my mind's eye.

I heard God whisper, 'Believe again.' I cried a little, mostly out of frustration, and complained to God that we tried three times and it didn't work. The word 'Faithful' flashed up into my mind's eye as I sobbed face down on our bed. In the past, I have believed and trusted people only to have that trust used against me. The request to 'believe again' goes against what I want, against what I feel capable of—even what I desire right now—but because you've told me to, God, I will obey. I will try not to grumble. I will trust you for as long as you want me to.

Thursday, 1 January 2015

Diary Entry

I am sitting in the lounge room, watching the sunrise. It's the first sunrise of the year. It's the first day of 2015. My spirit is engaged as I watch the beautiful pink sky change colour. Thank you, God for this beautiful new dawn.

'Forget about what's happened don't keep going over old history. Be alert, be present. I'm about to do something brand-new. It's bursting out! Don't you see it? There it is! I'm making a road through the desert and rivers in the badlands.' (Isaiah 43:19 MSG)

I felt drawn to work on the *Silver Lining* book. I could divide the book into three sections: First, the beginning of the triplets' lives; second, the loss of their lives; and third, our having another child. I'm still organizing my thoughts. We'll see how it all works out.

7

AUTUMN SIGHTINGS

Thursday, 5 February 2015

<u>Diary Entry</u>

One year ago today, our boys Summer, Snow, and Sky were born and went to heaven. I am grateful for the grace, strength, and hope God has given us to get through this tragedy. My heart is tender, but I also feel stronger, wiser, and more confident that no matter what life brings, God will help us through it.

A good friend of ours encouraged us in saying that God showed him that Ash and I are going to have more children and it's not something we need to worry about.

Sunday, 15 March 2015

<u>Diary Entry</u>

We had a wonderful pamper party. Wow! We raised more money than I expected for Orphancare Foundation in South Africa, to help the housemothers and to get more supplies for the babies they are caring for. Those housemothers go to great lengths to look after the babies, and like all loving parents, they regularly forget to look after themselves and to take care of their own needs. They selflessly care for abused and vulnerable babies that have been abandoned. We would love to do something special for them by sending them to a resort for a day of pampering. I have the most generous family and friends. I'm excited about blessing these precious women in South Africa.

As I counted the donated cash and sealed the envelope, I sensed a tingle of expectation and excitement about blessing these women. A collected effort was always much more rewarding, and our lives were filled with generous people who extended themselves to help those in need. Refreshed by the generosity of my family and friends, I researched retreats and day spas in Cape Town.

Sunday, 21 March 2015

<u>Diary Entry</u>

As I woke up early this morning, I heard God say, 'I will do it again.'

'Do what?' I asked curiously.

'Give you more children.'

The words lingered in my head for a while; then I went back to sleep. When I woke up later that morning, I sat listening for God's voice. This time I saw an image of three boys up on the top of a hill in the distance and two other children closer to me. They were wearing overalls. One had very curly hair.

God clearly said, 'Your children. With me all things are possible.'

I wrote down what I had heard and seen, and I then closed my journal.

Saturday, 4 April 2015

Diary Entry

> We are in Cape Town, South Africa. I can't believe it! We are back again, in the land of my birth! God, I pray that you help us in all that we need to do today.

I sank into my seat as I watched the bright flashes of colour blaze past as we drove along the damp road towards the south. These competitors of the Two Oceans Marathon had not given in to the wet climate but had faced the rain with determination. The clouds had not kept them from reaching their goals of participating; they had not dampened their spirits. I took courage from their example and mentally prepared myself for what lay ahead.

The charity that we support in Cape Town, had allocated the money that was donated by our family and friends to build a preschool on the property of a safe house for orphaned babies and children. We were on our way to visit the newly constructed preschool.

Ash and I were hoping to spend some private time in the preschool. After being admitted into the house, we were ushered past the children, who were enjoying their breakfast. Their excitement at seeing visitors was heart-warming, but we were mindful that our presence at that busy moment of the day was more of a distraction than help. We slipped out through the back door and entered the backyard. The housemother walked us to the side of the house and gestured towards the dark ochre building, situated securely on a red brick foundation that had become their new preschool.

Ash and I stepped closer to the building and were greeted with a colourful painted sign on the wall of the house, which read 'School of Miracles'. There was also a note painted next to the sign acknowledging Ash and me by name. The word 'miracle' hit me with an unexpected arrow of pain. We had believed for our own miracle. We had held on until the very last minute, but it was not to be. My mind raced back to the moment that I cried out for God's help in hospital more than a year before. The memory of longing for a divine intervention weighed down on me as I walked closer to the charming little preschool. I smiled as I tried desperately not to cry in the presence of the housemother. She invited us to enter the preschool; then she turned and walked back towards the safe house. Ash unlatched the horizontal split door and ushered me into the room. A clean, clear space greeted me as I scanned from the right to the left of the room. The perimeter of the room was lined with shelves of toy boxes and books, as well as small, colourful desks for the children. Some of the children's artwork and photos hung along one side of the room. It appeared to be an organized and happy place to learn. A poster with a quote from Nelson Mandela regarding education hung proudly near the teacher's resource corner.

In the solemn tour of this remarkable place, I could not help the emotions surfacing again. If it weren't for the lives of Summer, Snow, and Sky and the generosity of our family and friends, this place for educating vulnerable children would not exist. The preschoolers who grew, developed their skills, and learned new and wonderful things about the world would never know the three boys whose short lives gave them a chance to succeed.

Saturday, 23 May 2015

Diary Entry

> We are back from South Africa. The trip was incredible! We have so many fantastic stories of God helping us and guiding us. Thanks to the dreaded jet lag, I've been waking up at crazy o'clock and sleeping through the day. I think I may be ill. I'm hoping to stay in bed to rest up.

Tuesday, 26 May 2015

Diary Entry

> Thank you God, for a wonderful night's rest. I slept until 5.45 a.m. and didn't cough much last night. I slept like a baby. Feeling a lot better this morning. I think I'm ready to be kind. This morning I saw an image in my mind's eye of Ash and me having a picnic with our children. There were two.

Saturday, 30 May 2015

Diary Entry

> I made an appointment with our fertility specialist again. I am concerned about the meeting because I feel as if I will be placing myself in a vulnerable position emotionally by starting the process of ovulation induction again. Last year was a long and tiring process with no positive results. I am torn between these pervasive emotions and the contrasting pictures and words that God continues to give me about our future children. Ash has faith to believe God for this miracle, but I must admit that I am less confident. 'Trust in the Lord with all your heart and

lean not on your own understanding' (Proverbs 3:5 NIV). Trust is a decision. God will make my path straight if I trust Him. There are parts of our lives that are buried in mystery, but the reward comes if we trust Him before the answer to the mystery is revealed.

Monday, 29 June 2015

<u>Diary Entry</u>

It has been nearly a month since I wrote in my journal. This morning I was asked by God to wait quietly for a few minutes with my eyes closed. In my mind's eye, I saw Ash and me with our children on a white or cream-coloured couch. We were playing, laughing, and having fun.

I opened my eyes and thought about what I had just seen. Firstly, we didn't have a white or cream couch, and secondly, we didn't have living children. However, I trust that because God has shown me, He will bring it into reality sometime in the future.

Friday, 3 July 2015

<u>Diary Entry</u>

I decided to begin working on *Silver Lining: The Story of Summer, Snow, and Sky*. An uneasy but urgent sensation to begin this project looms as I think about how this will affect me. Will I be able to write what I feel clearly? Would it be painful to revisit those memories?

I created a new file on my laptop and began typing notes to include in the story. Recording our experience under separate categories, I typed notes about what it was like losing our triplets, and then how happily our story ended once we met our next child. This seemed like a premature thing to do, as we did not have any other children to speak of. And even though I had not seen the end of the story, I felt that if I wrote down what had happened so far, I could be ready to add the next part when God gave us a child or children. I knew there was something I needed to do before I could continue. There had been a tugging in my heart because I had neglected to take another important step in the process of my healing.

Hesitantly, I opened our study door and stared at the shelf to my left. There was a box containing precious items—namely the memory book of photos of the triplets after they were born that the hospital had given us. I had been avoiding this book, as I was scared of the effect those pictures would have on me. Cautiously lifting the lid of the box, I whispered a prayer for God to help me. I knew that opening this book was a huge step forward in my healing process, but it was not easy. The contrasting pounding of my heart against the stillness of the room forced me to fight to settle myself. I took a few slow, even breaths. The air in the room was still and stagnant. After staring at the box for a while, I prayed that this experience would not scar me emotionally. Visual memories had the tendency to stay in my mind and haunt me days, weeks, and even years later. Scared that this could create one of those memories, I stopped and contemplated my next step. As if I were handling an armed bomb, I opened the lid of the container and took a moment to breathe. Desperately trying to settle the anxious bubbling sensation in my belly, I intentionally relaxed the tension in my shoulders and neck. At a loss to remain calm, I decided that I already needed a break, as I could the sense the pressure of this situation releasing anxiety all too quickly. I walked out of the study to get a glass of water.

Thirty minutes later, I re-entered the room. Fortunately I was alone at home and could allow myself to react in whichever way I needed to. I lifted the glossy silver gift box out of the larger container. This was a gift from the funeral services. Inside the box was a beautiful blanket with the names of our boys embroidered on it. The tears began to flow. I smoothed my hand gently over their names. The pain in my chest was finally released by yet another gush of tears. I wiped my face. The lump in my throat was hard to swallow, so I closed my eyes and pressed the delicate blanket against my cheek for a few moments. Hot tears streamed down my face as I imagined a baby snuggled comfortably in this cocoon. Gently touching each of the name tags, which were placed around each of our triplet boys' ankles after they were born, I marvelled at how tiny their ankles were. The ribbons from the tags were so small that they could fit around my pinkie finger. With the blanket and the name tags having been returned to their original places in the box, I closed the lid. Blowing my nose and trying to compose myself for what came next, I repositioned myself on the carpeted floor. Under the silver gift box was a notebook which a kind friend of mine had given to me around the time of our loss. Inside the notebook was a memory book given to us by the hospital. I held the memory book close to my chest and wept for a while.

After the wave of emotion subsided, I held the book in both hands. Squinting my eyes while paging through for the first time because I was unsure of what I would see. My tears clouded my vision, so I wiped them away with the back of my hand, and then my eyes caught sight of a photo of our three beautiful boys. They looked so peaceful as they rested, their eyes closed and their heads covered with tiny knitted caps as they all lay wrapped snugly in fleecy blankets. I desperately searched their faces to see if there were any resemblances to Ash or me. They were absolutely adorable. They were real. They were precious. They were born too soon but were wonderfully made. My heart longed for them, longed to hear their voices, and longed to hear them cry. I wanted to see them open their eyes and look at me. *Did they know who I was?* I comforted myself that they could hear my voice while they were safe in my belly during my pregnancy. I once read that babies were able to hear and decipher a parent's voice from about sixteen weeks gestation. Our boys were at twenty weeks gestation, so surely our boys knew Ash's voice and mine. *Did they know what was happening when they were being born, or did God graciously protect them until their little spirits went to heaven?* I combed through the pages slowly and took in every detail of their sizes, weights, and lengths. I observed their tiny handprints and footprints, which the midwives had carefully arranged for us. I was so grateful to the hospital staff that preserved those treasurable memories on our behalf. In no condition to look at the boys straight after they were born, I would have missed this remarkable gift.

I was totally in love with my boys, and my heart was caught in a mixture of pain and joy. How beautiful they were, and yet how sad I was that I was never able to know them after they were born. Ash held them all in his arms. He sang over them. He told them that Mummy and Daddy loved them very much, and then they went to heaven. Each boy had a heartbeat when he was born. Summer, Snow, and Sky were our amazing gifts from God.

To think that some babies this age or older who are healthy are not allowed to live broke my heart. Of course, I do not judge anyone who has had an abortion; I am aware that people face all kinds of challenges and difficulties when expecting a child. But looking at those pictures, I felt sore in my heart for those who find themselves in a situation in which the only option they see is termination. I believe that the complexities of life mean that nothing is simply black and white, but it upset me that many babies that are conceived do not live through to birth.

My heart ached for the children that would never live long enough to take their first breaths of air; to enjoy the comfort and love from nursing at their mothers' breasts or lying in their mothers' arms; to bond with their mothers and fathers; to open their eyes outside the womb; to experience this big, unfamiliar world; to smell, feel, taste, and hear, to grow into children and then into adults; to develop; to learn; to experience; and to enjoy. My heart broke for babies like ours, who came too soon, and for all parents who had lost a child.

Gazing, exploring, and marvelling at the photos repeatedly, I felt relieved. *Why had I been so afraid to see them?* These were our children, and I loved them with my whole heart. I felt God healing me as I wept. This whole experience proved not scary or scarring, but cathartic. I closed the book, packed away all of these precious items, and thanked God for our dear children.

Cape Town at dawn.

8

WINTER WORRIES

Thursday, 13 August 2015

<u>Diary Entry</u>

> I got a call from our fertility specialist's office a few days ago regarding a small procedure that I need to have, which will hopefully help me with conceiving. It will be done in hospital, and I need to go under general anaesthetic. I have an appointment at the hospital today. I got up at 6.30 a.m. but couldn't have breakfast.

As I sat in the waiting room of the hospital, I thought about what my day had in store. My stomach felt a little strange, and I couldn't decide whether it was because I had been told not to eat or drink anything after midnight or whether it was because I was nervous. Voices chattered in the distance, machines beeped, and television noises played the news of the day quietly in the background. I decided to journal, but I did not have any words to write, so I turned to the brochures I had received from the kind nurse as I entered the reception area. My fertility specialist doctor and nurse had explained the whole procedure to me in a few different ways, but I flicked through the glossy pages to see whether they mentioned anything about trying to remain calm and positive about this operation. As I was being ushered into another waiting room, the nurse explained that I needed to change into the hospital gown, cap, and slippers in the bathroom and then proceed to the next waiting room.

Moments later, I emerged from the bathroom feeling vulnerable in my operation ensemble and made my way to the available chair in the waiting room. With a quick glance at the couple to my left as I entered the room, I could see that the female looked equally as uncomfortable in the outfit that the hospital had provided for her. Encouragingly I offered a smile, and she smiled back but then quickly looked down towards her slippers as I passed her seat.

Then I waited. There were several other people waiting behind curtained areas in that room. From the conversations with the nursing staff, I understood that each of those patients behind the curtained areas was in post-operation recovery. No one seemed too upset, which gave me hope that this procedure could not possibly be as bad as I anticipated.

Over an hour later, my name was called and I was transferred to yet another room. The nurses I met in this room seemed enthusiastic about their job. They asked me a series of questions about allergies and my general health, and they checked other information on the form I had filled in earlier. The nurse offered me help in settling onto the hospital bed as the anaesthetist instructed me to count backwards from ten. I started, and within seconds I could feel myself become drowsy.

Groggily opening my eyes, I heard the voice of my doctor. She touched my arm and spoke my name a few times. Leaning down over me with a smile on her face, she told me that it all went to plan and that I should rest. Like a dream, I floated back to sleep after her last word.

Numerous machine beeps and distant chatter in the hospital ward woke me again. As I sat up, dizziness overcame me and I nearly passed out. The nurse advised me to lie back down, and they took my blood pressure reading.

Later Ash called my phone, and I explained to him that I was still recovering. A few hours later, the doctor in charge of the ward and a few nurses discussed my recovery progress and informed me that I was unable to go home as I was still very weak and my blood pressure was very low. I continued drinking the water they provided.

Weary and weak, I slept for another few hours. The next time I woke up, the doctor informed me that my blood pressure had improved and I was able to move to the next waiting area, so I slowly changed back into my clothing and shoes. The medical staff were still waiting for me to show signs of full recovery before they were comfortable with me leaving the hospital. The curette and laparoscope, or 'golf-balling', procedures that I had just undergone were meant to aid my ability to conceive. I tried not to focus on the ache I felt in my abdomen but rather turned my attention to the potential that this procedure promised.

A friend joined me in hospital, as Ash was still at work. It had now been nearly twelve hours since I arrived. I was told that if I did not improve, I would be encouraged to stay overnight. My friend and I said a quiet prayer, and she cheered me up with encouragement, kind words, and thoughtful gifts.

I was finally discharged. Grateful to the wonderful staff at the hospital for showing me extra care and help when I needed it most, I thanked each one as I began preparing to leave. I relaxed in the waiting room until Ash arrived. He drove me home, checking regularly that I was completely comfortable.

9

SHARING IN SPRING

Friday, 11 September 2015

<u>Diary Entry</u>

I had a pretty tough day. Ash encouraged me. Before I went to sleep, he read the story of Gideon from the Bible (Judges chapters 6 and 7 NIV). It was a massive blessing. Thank you, God, for this amazing husband!

Monday, 14 September 2015

<u>Diary Entry</u>

Today is a beautiful day. Our home is quiet at the moment. My spirit, body, and soul are still and at peace. I get the sense that God is going to transform our house into a place of children's laughter!

Friday, 2 October 2015

<u>Diary Entry</u>

In the past week, I've had to avoid a few conversations with people about whether or not Ash and I will be trying for another child. Talking about this sensitive issue is not one that I relish. These moments are difficult because of the discomfort of telling people that we are going through processes to enable me to have a better chance of becoming pregnant. My reason for withholding this news is mainly because I do not want to raise people's hopes or open it up to further conversations about this topic. I am struggling with this already and trying desperately to avoid the added pressure of people's expectations.

Tuesday, 20 October 2015

<u>Diary Entry</u>

Ash and I dropped a cradle, and a few other baby-related supplies at a mutual friend's home. They had just had a little boy. He was small and fragile but beautiful. The family invited us to stay for afternoon tea, and we felt like the kind thing to do would be to take them up on their invitation.

Thursday, 22 October 2015

<u>Diary Entry</u>

God, please give us a child that will live to honour you, a miracle baby that will always be a reminder of your goodness in our lives. I believe that God is willing for me to become pregnant. This could happen without medical assistance, or it could happen as a result of brilliantly competent doctors and medical staff. Either way, God chooses. I trust that it will happen in His way and in His timing! In my journal I made a list of all the times that God has answered my prayers recently. The list is very long!

Saturday, 31 October 2015

Diary Entry

> We arrived at Howqua River yesterday just after 3.00 p.m., set up camp, and stopped only for an afternoon snack. Our extended family who regularly camp with us joined us. We helped them set up camp, and then we all started making dinner.

Camping had always been one of my favourite pastimes. I grew up camping during holiday periods with my immediate and extended families both in South Africa and Australia. Although camping without running water or electricity seemed like a lot of extra work, I always felt energized by our trips. This was because we were close to nature and perhaps because this way of living reminded me of how fortunate I was to have amenities and other luxuries at home. The slower pace of life could be another reason, as could the fact that we were cut off from all outside communication, including the Internet, social media, and the like. Camping was usually a time when Ash and I discussed our goals, plans, and what we believed God was saying to us.

Diary Entry

> I am sitting in the caravan, looking out the window. It is serene and peaceful in this place. All I can hear are the birds singing sweetly, a few voices chatting quietly from another campsite, and a dog barking intermittently in the distance.

One thing I was looking forward to was taking our child camping and making this a frequent part of our holidays together. There were many things to teach our future child about a camping holiday. I sat and thought for a while about how much fun it would be to see our child discover new and interesting things in his or her world. We watched our relatives closely over the years and admired how relaxed and open they were about allowing their children to have new experiences in nature and how to become more hardy and resilient.

Monday, 2 November 2015

<u>Diary Entry</u>

> The rain woke us up this morning, but then the sun came up and dried everything. Now I can see that it is going to be a wonderfully sunny day.

Engaged in reading an intriguing novel, I enjoyed the warmth of the sun and tried to decide whether or not I would swim. Water activity had always been another favourite pastime of mine since I was very young. My parents often refereed to me as a 'fish' whenever we were near a body of water, because of my love of swimming. I hoped our children would be the same. Having completed my swimming teaching certificate, I felt confident that I could teach them to enjoy the water from a very young age.

The water was cool and refreshing, and I was pleased with my decision to swim. I scooped the water into my cupped hands, lifted it and poured it over my hair and face, and then decided to immerse the rest of my body. *Is there anything better than swimming on a scorching, dry day?* It was only spring, but the weather was hot enough to convince me that it was already summer. I wondered whether we would become pregnant in summer. As I floated on my back, I stared up at the blue sky and counted the nine months in my head. *If we became pregnant in December, I could give birth next September.* A spring baby sounded good. However, if it happened in March or even April, we would have a baby in summer. As I treaded water, I thought of how much fun it would be to swim with our darling. I said a quick prayer as I continued to dream about our future child. Only God knew what the future held.

Friday, 20 November 2015

Diary Entry

> Ash and I celebrate our wedding anniversary today! Thank you, God, for this incredible man! I love being his wife! Ash and I are convinced that God wants us to go to South Africa for six months next year.

The plans for living in South Africa had suddenly come alive. Some of our extended family had agreed to move into the house we are currently living in. We were excited about seeing our South African family and friends again. Also, our plans included volunteering and helping vulnerable young women.

Monday, 30 November 2015

Diary Entry

> I had the strangest dream that I was at Ma and Pa's house. I was learning how to breastfeed a new baby. I felt calm and safe in that space, holding my treasured child.

What was that dream really about? I could not put my finger on it, but I was irritated by this dream. With thoughts swirling in my mind, I struggled to push away the images from that dream as I climbed back into bed a few minutes later. Pondering the symbolic nature of where I was in the dream, whom I was with, and what was happening in the dream, I came to this conclusion: I suppose my grandparent's house symbolized home to me. It had always been a safe and nurturing place. Perhaps I was longing to experience motherhood in a place where I was nurtured as a child. However, there was uneasiness in my heart, a longing unfulfilled, and a troubled mind. *Why did I long so much for the day that I would be able to hold my own child? Why did I have such an ache in my heart every time I thought of what it would be like if I never had this opportunity?*

Restless, I grappled with my thoughts about this topic for the next two hours. Anxiety rose in me as I contemplated a life without children, a life without our next generation, a life without the experience of motherhood. My heart ached, and my tension turned to tears. My tears led me back to sleep, but this time I could not remember my dreams when I awoke.

Monday, 21 December 2015

<u>Diary Entry</u>

> Thank you, God, for a fantastic holiday! We drove to NSW for a pre-Christmas family holiday. Jervis Bay is beautiful!

Time spent with our extended family was both refreshing and strengthening. I was grateful for each member who enriched our lives with their unique individual personalities.

This place must resemble paradise, I thought as I sat on the beach under the clear sky, staring out at the glassy aqua water. Two of my nieces were swimming with their parents, my mother was resting on her beach chair, Ash was enjoying the coolness of the waves, my brother was resting in the shade, and my third niece was next to me, covering her legs with sand.

Wiping a bug from my legs, I looked up to see others also enjoying the refreshing cool water. Today, although I was enjoying the time with my family, I began to dread the upcoming Christmas celebrations. Even though I vowed that I would enjoy Christmas and make every effort to change my attitude to a positive one, Christmas time reminded me of what we had lost. It would have been our triplets' second Christmas. Sure, they may have been too young to know what was going on, but what a wonderful time we could have shared with all three of them. The emotions welled up into my throat, and I discreetly wiped the tears from behind my sunglasses.

<u>Diary Entry</u>

> I cried out to God about losing our boys. It has definitely left a hole in our lives. I see an image in my mind's eye of Ash and me carrying something wrapped in a blanket. It looks like a newborn baby.

I opened to the book of Isaiah in the Bible and read this verse: 'See I am doing a new thing! Now it springs up; do you not perceive it? I am making a way in the wilderness and streams in the wasteland' (Isaiah 43:19 NIV).

As I reread this passage several times, I wept quietly, holding on to the hope that God was able to do a new thing in us.

10

SUMMER IN THE SUN

Monday, 28 December 2015

<u>Diary Entry</u>

> I had a strange dream that Ash and I went to the beach
> and walked until we reached the car park of a shopping
> centre. We then took a bus home. I noticed that Ash was
> holding a little baby. The baby had curly hair like one of
> our nieces. I woke up feeling hopeful.

As I regained my composure later that morning whilst eating
breakfast, I pondered the dream. *Could this mean that our child
will have curly hair?* These dreams were bittersweet because they
brought hope for a moment but left me with a fresh reminder of
my longing to be a mother.

Saturday, 16 January 2016

<u>Diary Entry</u>

> God, thank you for SCKC and for being part of this truly
> wonderful experience. You led me to it, and you made a

way. You helped me. You provided for me and grew me through this experience.

My role as camp counsellor for an organization which conducts camps for vulnerable children in our community was both an honour and a privilege. Those precious children were never the same after these camps. The members of the organization went to great lengths to make the camping trip the most fulfilling and encouraging experience. The volunteers were fun-loving, patient, kind, enthusiastic, creative role models who were dedicated to making a positive difference in those children's lives. The week away was rewarding in many ways. It reminded me that even with all my struggles, I was extremely fortunate to have family and friends who cared for me. After camp, I was usually sleep-deprived, but I was filled with passion to help again the next year.

Sunday, 17 January 2016

Diary Entry

Ash and I believe that this part of our journey includes a six-month trip to South Africa to volunteer and to visit family. We are also hoping to launch my album *Finding Me* while we are there.

Thursday, 4 February 2016

Diary Entry

Ash and I had a listening party yesterday in the studio. Our album is done, thanks to our producer and executive producer! I love listening to our songs!

Saturday, 20 February 2016

Diary Entry

We received news that friends of ours had twin boys.
We are so happy for them. Maybe our children will play
together one day.

11

AUTUMN IN AFRICA

Monday, 11 April 2016

<u>Diary Entry</u>

Today I attended the Hillsong Colour Conference in Cape Town. During the praise and worship session, I saw an image of an ultrasound with the profile of a baby. I had my eyes closed but could see the image of the ultrasound in my mind's eye as clearly as if it were being held up in front of my face.

Wednesday, 27 April 2016

<u>Diary Entry</u>

It's Freedom Day in South Africa. Thank you, God, for those who sacrificed so that we could have political and social freedom! And thank you, Jesus, for your ultimate sacrifice so that we could have every freedom!

As I leaned across the couch and straightened the bedsheet I thought about what freedom meant to me. Many years ago, my grandfather's cousin Eddie Daniels was imprisoned for standing against racism in South Africa. We had the great honour of meeting Eddie in 2015 and were amazed to find no bitterness in his heart. For someone who had suffered such great injustices, lost years with his own children and wife, and survived years in prison enduring the harsh treatment on Robben Island, he appeared to have nothing but forgiveness for his captives and those who were responsible for placing him in that prison.

Eddie Daniels's example taught me that when injustice is present, it is our responsibility to stand up on behalf of the victim and to use what we have been given to help others. His life was one of sacrifice for the benefit of others. He saw that life was not fair for some people in his country, so he decided to do something about it. His legacy will live on in my life and in the lives of my family members. My courage to speak up for those who cannot speak for themselves in my volunteer work with orphans and vulnerable youth was, in part, a result of the inspiration drawn from his life.

Friday, 20 May 2016

Diary Entry

> Today I sang my song 'Princess' for a group of girls at one of the children's homes. As I sang the words 'Put on your crown again Princess', I could feel the atmosphere in the room changing in a positive way. The programmes are running well, and the girls seem to be enjoying each session. We are very close to releasing the album *Finding Me*.

After saying goodbye to the girls at the gate of the safe home, I stepped back into the car. What a change in their attitudes from that first moment we arrived only a few weeks earlier. The girls seemed cold and abrasive during that first session, and I struggled to stay focused on running the programme in the sequence I was accustomed to. Their responses to my questions and requests for participation were brief or sometimes non-existent. After several attempts at trying to build rapport that very first day, I decided to tell parts of my own story, which brought an instant change in the atmosphere in the room. Some of the girls who had previously avoided eye contact with me could fight it no longer and engaged with every word I spoke for the rest of the session. When I told of my own struggles with abuse, family violence, bullying, and an eating disorder, their attitudes appeared to melt away, and what was left were vulnerable girls who had witnessed and experienced far too much pain at their tender age. With every new session, the girls opened up and told of some of their personal struggles. I tried to create a safe space for them, and even though it was clear that there were deep wounds in many of their lives, they appeared to be shifting into hope. Those sessions left me feeling helpless, angry on their behalf, humbled, but hopeful. As much as those girls were grateful for my efforts in running the programmes with them, it was clear to me that they also helped me. They listened to my stories, they opened their hearts during our discussions, they accepted my advice, they shared affectionate words, and, despite what many of them had suffered, they showed gratitude.

As I read through their final comments about their experience in our sessions, I was moved to tears. The most impacting aspect of the programme was when they realized that because of my own experiences as a South African girl, I was attuned to their suffering and, with help, was able to heal and flourish. I believed change came by being able to show empathy and allowing them to explore the possibility of hope despite their struggles. Helping others find truth and courage, by sharing my story, fostered part of my own healing process.

Diary Entry

> Encouragement is like oxygen. When I give others encouraging words, it's like putting an oxygen mask on them and one on myself. They are revived, boosted, lifted, and strengthened, but I, too, benefit from that oxygen.

Wednesday, 25 May 2016

Diary Entry

> Another friend of mine had twins. I am happy for her and her husband. It's becoming easier to celebrate with those who have children. Thank you, God. This is evidence of your healing in my heart. I'm so grateful for your goodness in my life!

Thursday, 26 May 2016

Diary Entry

> It's happening! The album *Finding Me* by L. A. Field (me) is available as a pre-release! The whole album will be out on the tenth of June! This is a dream come true! We have been working on this album for years! I remind myself that good things come to those who wait! We could not have done it without our wonderful producer who worked tirelessly on it from the beginning to end.

Saturday, 28 May 2016

<u>Diary Entry</u>

> My beautiful and talented aunt cooked a meal for the
> dinner party we are hosting for some friends. The couple
> visiting us have had their own struggles with starting a
> family, but they have a strong faith that God will give
> them a child. We talked until the early hours of the
> morning, and although my body was tired, my spirit
> was soaring.

At the end of our conversation, we prayed for each other. My
friend made a comment about looking forward to our children
playing together in the future. In the moment, I almost missed her
comment, but her words rang in my ears until I drifted off to sleep.

Table Mountain, Cape Town.

12

WORSHIP IN WINTER

Wednesday, 1 June 2016

<u>Diary Entry</u>

> I heard that a couple we know well lost a baby this week.
> My heart broke for them. I will pray for them. The first
> day of winter is always a difficult time for me, as it marks
> the day that my grandmother went to heaven. She passed
> away five years ago—five long years ago. I went to bed
> early last night but had restless sleep. I woke up at 3.36
> a.m., dozed until 6.52 a.m., and then decided to get out
> of bed.

I brooded about the miserable start to my day as I began writing
in my journal. Then I remembered that it was up to me to decide
how this day would develop. I had a choice. I could either give
negativity a voice or I could scream positivity in everything I said
and did. One of the key things I found that helped me during those
cloudy, emotional days was finding positive words from songs,
stories, podcasts, and books to absorb into my heart and mind.
My decision to be proactive in the choices which consumed my
mental and emotional energy paid off, and I ended my day feeling

strong. This has taken me years to learn, and I didn't always get it right, but what a joy it was to my soul when I chose what was best.

Tuesday, 12 July 2016

Diary Entry

> I woke up around 3.00 a.m. this morning and had a crazy dream that Ash and I were the parents of twins. We took them home and started taking care of them.

My conviction was that dreams had the power to take a very strong hold on my thoughts and emotions. The feeling of having something beautiful and satisfying in the dream only to realize once I woke up that it was not real was deflating. Those post-dream moments were crushing, and I was struggling to resist the temptation to allow the dreams to affect my entire days.

Monday, 18 July 2016

Diary Entry

> It feels good to be back in Cape Town. This really is our second home.

During the singing at our church evening service, I sat on my seat and closed my eyes, even though my usual custom was to sing together with the rest of the congregation. Worship services drew me in to a place where I met with God in a very special way. Today I felt weariness settle over me, so I decided to rest. I allowed those around me to sing because I was emotionally unable to. I heard the woman behind me, her voice gently drifting over me. As I continued to listen, I heard the lady sitting on my left singing powerfully and adding her own beautiful melodies to create an even more glorious sound. The lady to my right also sang sweetly, but she sang softly. I felt enveloped by the power of passionate song. Taking a deep breath, I relaxed into my chair even further. The singing, mingled with a cacophony of other voices and instruments, brought me a deep sense of peace and safety. Their voices wooed me along to join in the chorus of praise to my God. In this state of complete ease, I heard God speaking to me and encouraging me. I sensed God's love and comfort. I sensed His hope. I shed some tears and asked Him to help me to hold on to faith. I found myself rocking gently to and fro to the rhythm of the music. As I stood up from my seat a few minutes later, I felt stronger.

In contrast to this serene evening, Ash and I drove past several sex workers on our way back to our apartment. I looked out at each of these women as we passed them along the main road. The sun had set, but I could still manage to see their faces. I found myself profoundly moved by how young they all looked. I caught the eye of one of the girls as we stopped at the traffic lights. She stared at me without moving at all. I smiled, but it was as if I were staring at a statue. There was no expression on her beautiful but wearied face, and the emptiness in her eyes were haunting. I turned away, and sadness rose up in my chest and flashed across my face, producing tears. These were also God's precious daughters. The traffic lights changed, and we drove on.

Confronted and in shock, I sat still, unsure how to articulate what I had just experienced. Closing my eyes again, I tried to picture their faces. I prayed silently for each of those precious women, knowing in my heart that something must be done to help them.

Wednesday, 10 August 2016

<u>Diary Entry</u>

> The view from Lion's Head in Cape Town South Africa
> is breathtaking.

This was not the first time we had been on top of this beautiful landmark over the past few years. Being able to see Table Mountain, the city, and the ocean from this angle was truly awe-inspiring.

I nearly made it all the way up Lion's Head without stopping. I sat on a rock and took in every inch of my view. Noticing the houses, buildings, cars, and trees in the distance, I composed myself and then stood up. The air filled my lungs, and I felt the breeze across the dried sweat on my forehead and along my temples. This was a stunning view, and was definitely worth the climb. My hands were hot, and the skin on my fingers felt stretched.

Ash, I, and a good friend of ours stood and watched the sunrise across the city over the Hottentots Holland Mountains. The city of my birth was one of exquisite beauty. It could be troubled and unsafe at times, but my love for this place kept growing. Each time we visited Cape Town, I fell more and more in love with it: the people, the landscape, the animals, the food, the music, the culture, the scars of history, and the bittersweet memories of my adventures as a child. It was difficult to describe exactly what moved me so much about this place, but it could be something to do with my heritage. I sensed myself being knitted into the fabric of this town's past and future. The prayer and passion invested in South Africa through some of my own relatives would live on for generations to come.

That evening, as I prepared for the school programme for the next day, I noticed how sore and tender my muscles were. The impact of the mountain climb manifested through the pain and aches in my body. I fought with the temptation to postpone the following day's session. I summoned my energy and focused on the reason I was going to meet with them. When my feelings and energy came up short, my passion kicked in. I focused on what was important: sharing my story and telling all of these girls that they were unique, valued, and loved.

13

ANOTHER SPRING BEGINS

Monday, 12 September 2016

<u>Diary Entry</u>

God has already done so much of what He promised to do on this trip. When our time is up, we can leave Cape Town satisfied and thankful. I love my relationship with God. It's absolutely amazing. He loves me so much! I'm very grateful for that love.

Wednesday, 21 September 2016

<u>Diary Entry</u>

As I sang along with the other people in the music workshop this morning, I saw an image. There was a long, white hallway. White walls were everywhere. There was a passageway leading to an opening. God called me closer, and I continued to walk down the passage. I had a blue baby blanket in my hand. My healing had definitely progressed, as this kind of image would have undone me for days in the past. However, now my process included sensing the emotions in a real and raw way, and then moving on into hope. I usually left my experience feeling lighter—still tender, but grateful for what I had.

Later that day, as I reflected on the image, my emotions stirred deep within. After writing in my journal, I reclined on the bed and wiped my tears, blew my nose, and took a sip of water from my water bottle. I stared at the words that I had penned in my journal. I did not know how people healed from the loss of a child without a relationship with God. There was such a hollowness that lingered with this loss. I'd had many losses in my life, but this one had almost broken me. If it were not for my relationship with God, the love of my husband, the kindness of my family and friends, and my hope in an eternal future, I am not sure how I would have coped.

Thursday, 22 September 2016

Diary Entry

I felt encouraged as I meditated and listened to God's still, small voice. With music playing in the background, I sense my spirit lift.

Music had been an important catalyst in my healing process. Cautious in my selection of songs, I allowed my spirit to absorb the words, which reframed my thoughts and lifted my emotions so that pain was able to leave and gratitude was invited to enter. My default in the past was to avoid the painful issues, contain my emotions, and mask them by finding comfort in unhealthy or unhelpful sources. Although I had not mastered my management of grief, I believed that I was learning to be brave. As I asked God to search my heart, I found the areas that I had withdrawn from and shut off. From this place of safety with God, I learned to deal with each part as it surfaced.

Talking to others and praying with others was also an effective way of releasing those barbs from my past. Meditating on the promises in the Bible about my situation, I allowed truth to settle in my spirit as it flowed from my head to my heart and out through my words and actions.

With God's help, my story was one of triumph. My adolescent years spiralled out of control to the point where my pain was so severe that I wanted to end my life. I did not feel brave enough to confide in anyone back in those days. The weight of this secret crushed my spirit. It lured me from flirting with the idea for many months to eventually devising a plan. The reason I did not give in to this temptation and am still breathing and alive, is prayers spoken on my behalf. The demonstration of love from my family and friends allowed God's Spirit to lead me to a place of salvation, truth, and hope in Jesus Christ.

Another reason was linked to the responsibility I felt for looking after my younger brothers and sister. Although I was never perfect in my role as the eldest sister, I tried to salvage some peace and manage the toxic environment of our home. Many petitions in prayer for the violence to cease were expressed throughout my childhood. I dreamed of a peaceful home where life was filled with possibility.

As I thought back on this part of my life, I could still remember back to those pleas for peace, and all things considered, I was now living the dream. God's Spirit was evidently present in my life. He had proven time and time again to provide for me when I showed Him that I trusted Him. He continually drew people and opportunities to me that built me and strengthened my character.

God had given me a husband who loved me, walked in wisdom, worked hard to provide for me, respected me, and exuded joy. Our home was a home of peace. Our lives were full and flourishing not only in material things but also in the things that mattered most— the good stuff in life, such as acceptance, kindness, laughter, empathy, peace, compassion, expectation, hope, intimacy, and creativity.

My heart oozed with gratitude for God's unconditional love. No matter what the past had presented, I reminded myself that God had good things stored up for all and welcomed me to a life of love and adventure with Him.

Tuesday, 4 October 2016

Diary Entry

> Ash and I had discussed being grateful for what God has done in the past six months and were looking forward to what He was going to do. We started planning. As we said our goodbyes in South Africa, we received many encouragements around being expectant and knowing that God was excited for this next part of our journey. A good friend and leader in the church told us he believed that God was turning a new page for us. Ash and I took that encouragement and felt strengthened by his words.

Tuesday, 11 October 2016

Diary Entry

> We have arrived back in Australia. Thank you, God, for a safe journey back to Melbourne.

Reflecting on our experience in South Africa, I filled my journal with some of the wonderful things that Ash and I experienced. Life is certainly an adventure if you're willing to take a few risks.

My grandfather graciously allowed us to stay with him while we searched for a new home. Ash returned to work, while I settled back into my everyday routine. In the evenings, we drove around to look at available properties. We decided to go ahead with another fertility cycle. Although I had reservations, I took some comfort in the thought that it could take years for us to reach the perfect conditions for conceiving, based on our last experiences with the FSH ovulation induction process. The fertility nurse explained that even if I was able to ovulate and conceive, they were concerned that I may become pregnant with multiples again. This was problematic, as my body might not be capable of successfully carrying a multiple pregnancy through to a safe delivery date. Whenever I began to think about the possibilities of a repeat of our experience with the triplets, the fear rose in my heart and I began to dread any further proceedings.

Ash was a wonderful support, as he reminded me that God had promised to give us a child or even children one day. He urged me not to give up, and after a few minutes of listening to him, I was less fearful.

Thursday, 13 October 2016

<u>Diary Entry</u>

> I've had a blood test to check whether my thyroid has been functioning normally. I called the fertility nurse, and she said that it was normal. She instructed me to begin taking the tablets to start my menstrual cycle. I was to book an ultrasound appointment and then start

injections. I felt overwhelmed, so I spent some time talking to God and asked for His help. 'God, please have your way. I will step out in faith because it pleases you. We commit our plans for trying to conceive and have a baby to you.'

As I waited and meditated on the possibilities, the words from Isaiah 43 popped into my mind: 'Forget the former things; do not dwell on the past. See I am doing a new thing' (Isaiah 43:18 NIV).

I closed my eyes, took a deep breath, released the anxiety as I exhaled, and breathed in possibility.

Sunday, 16 October 2016

<u>Diary Entry</u>

In prayer and meditation this morning, I heard the phrase 'Change is coming'.

I have been invited to a baby shower. Wrestling with whether or not I am able to attend the event, I became a little emotional. After a few moments, I wrote this reflection: 'God, you have created every life. I look forward to the day that we will celebrate another life that you produce through us.'

I went to my cousin's baby shower today. I dearly love my family, but this was a particularly difficult event for me to attend. Pushing my own emotions aside, I chose to celebrate with all of them. Another relative at the baby shower was very kind to me, as she had been through a similar journey and was able to empathize with me right there in the moment. This was the first time I had been to a baby shower since we lost our triplets.

Initially I found myself relaxing and enjoying the time together, reconnecting with my relatives. After many conversations about babies and the joy of motherhood, I needed some air, so I escaped to the public toilets of the venue. The feelings of frustration regarding our predicament in not being able to conceive resurfaced. *Why was it so hard for us to start a family?* I asked God to help me as I whispered prayers between quiet sobs. I took out my mirror and was horrified at the appearance of the smeared mascara across my eyes and cheeks, and I quickly cleared it away with my last clean tissue. I began to flick through the apps on my phone. I settled on a real estate app and began looking for potential homes for rent. After I regained my composure, I reluctantly decided that my time of hiding out had come to an end.

Slowly rising to my feet, I opened the toilet lid, and threw the used tissues into the bowl, and then flushed them away. Strangely, watching the running water take the tissues was comforting.

Friday, 28 October 2016

Diary Entry

> So much has happened in a week. Prayer really does work. Ash and I are moving in a few days, I have accepted the full-time teaching position at a local school, and the training night for a charity that works with vulnerable children went exceptionally well.

Wednesday, 2 November 2016

<u>Diary Entry</u>

> We moved into our new place on Monday. Our family and friends rallied around us to help us with the mammoth task. I was exhausted but thrilled that everything went so smoothly. Yesterday I had a catch-up with my best friend. We regularly meet together to pray for each other.

Five years ago, I had a vision while I was praying that I was at my best friend's wedding. I was making a speech and had a pregnant belly. Many times I had pondered this vision when things in the baby-making department seemed grim. My anything-is-possible attitude would kick in, and I would be able to believe again. As we prayed together, she encouraged me to believe that all the effort, worry, and waiting would be worth it.

In the midst of reading a book about prayer, the author recounted her personal experiences of losing babies through miscarriages and stillborn births. Those losses made me incredibly angry. Why do innocent babies die? The author reframed her experiences in the idea that although God did not cause those deaths, He allowed her to use the pain to help others who were suffering or had suffered loss. So far this book had been an incredible blessing of encouragement and insight for me.

After reading this lady's story, I decided that I wanted to be a source of strength and encouragement to others who had faced a similar loss. I focused my attention towards writing my book, *Silver Lining*.

Wednesday, 9 November 2016

Diary Entry

Ash and I discussed the next step in the ovulation induction process. I am supposed to have another ultrasound scan and then go ahead with the FSH injections. Our fertility doctors and nurses are terrific. They support us through every step of this process, and we are grateful for their knowledge, expertise, and care. Ash and I talked about the next step in the process of conceiving, and we came to the conclusion that we would try a cycle.

Sunday, 13 November 2016

Diary Entry

This morning I found my journals and started collating and writing more in the Silver Lining manuscript. I looked at the pictures of Summer, Snow, and Sky again. They were so beautiful! I couldn't help but cry when I saw their tiny footprints in the book we received from the hospital. Thank you for our precious boys, and thank you again, God, for the people who preserved those memories for us.

Tuesday, 15 November 2016

Diary Entry

I had a fantastic day teaching yesterday. I received an encouragement award from the students. I was so touched! After dinner, Ash and I discussed adoption. I did some research on the Australian government's website. We believe we will have our own children, but it doesn't hurt to look into adoption too.

Thursday, 17 November 2016

Diary Entry

> I had a hectic day teaching. I am struggling with the process, as my body is preparing for this cycle. I am more irritable than I thought I would be. I have not started injections yet, as I am waiting to talk to our fertility doctor about the dosage.

Saturday, 19 November 2016

Diary Entry

> I had my second injection today. It didn't hurt at all.

As I prepared for my injection, I pressed play for the song on my phone and took out the needle. I dreaded each time I had to do this, but I knew that the discomfort did not last for long. As soon as self-pity tried to creep in, I reminded myself that millions of people who suffered from diabetes had no choice but to use needles every day just to stay alive. To make the process a more pleasurable one, I rewarded myself with a cup of tea and a biscuit after I put the medication back in the fridge. As I closed the fridge door, I thought, *another injection down*. Feeling relieved, as a student might after completing a homework assignment or project, I flopped down onto the couch and prepared for a rest.

Sunday, 20 November 2016

<u>Diary Entry</u>

Ash and I are heading to the beach to enjoy our traditional fish and chips meal. I love the beach. It is one place where I always find peace. The sand between my toes, the view of the ocean stretching out for many kilometres, the sound of the water crashing onto the beach, the fragrant fresh air, the feeling of the cool breeze blowing over me, the free feeling of the open space, and even the seagulls that frolic along the sandy beach brings me to a place of inner tranquillity.

We headed home after watching a beautiful sunset over the water, feeling contented, satisfied, and relaxed as we drove together. I felt that Ash was truly a gift to me. I could not imagine my life without him. I reached over to touch his hand, which was resting on the gear lever, and smiled at him. He responded to my affection. I breathed out and relaxed further into the seat as we drove on.

<u>Diary Entry</u>

I had my third Gonal F pen injection. Tonight will be my fourth injection, and then I will have a blood test tomorrow morning, first thing.

What I believe will happen in this coming year: teaching full-time, buying another car, promoting *Finding Me*, and maybe having a baby in 2018.

I read this verse: 'He settles the childless woman in her home as a happy mother of children' (Psalm 113:9 NIV).

Who were the women in the Bible who were childless for a season?
I recalled Rebekah, Rachel, Sarah, Manoah's wife, Elizabeth, and
the Shunammite woman. Those women struggled as they waited
for God to bring their promise into reality. Reading through the
stories of all of these women in the Bible and their experiences of
being barren encouraged me as they trusted God in their battles.

Tuesday, 22 November 2016

<u>Diary Entry</u>

I had a fairly productive day at home. I went for a blood
test at Melbourne Pathology and then came home, had
breakfast, and waited for Ash to get up. I received a call
from the fertility nurse, and she told me to take another
dose of FSH. She said she would call me in the morning.
I decided to work on my manuscript for *Silver Lining.*

Wednesday, 23 November 2016

<u>Diary Entry</u>

I had an ultrasound scan in Box Hill today. After
reviewing the results of the scan, our doctor suggested
that we lower the dosage amount and have another scan
on Thursday. I have one large follicle, two medium-sized
follicles, and three smaller follicles. This could land us in
the same place as before with the triplets, as some or all
of those eggs could be fertilized.

Thursday, 24 November 2016

<u>Diary Entry</u>

> I had another scan today. I have five potential fertilizing follicles, so our doctor did not want us to go ahead with this cycle. Frustrated that I could not see a way ahead, I felt as if we were back where we were three years ago.

Saturday, 26 November 2016

<u>Diary Entry</u>

> Ash and I discussed the next step of the process with our doctor, and she explained that my body responded very powerfully to the FSH hormones. She advised us not to go ahead, because with my history, all the follicles could take to the ovulation process and we could end up with multiples again.

I opened my Bible to Isaiah and read, 'Instead of your shame you will receive a double portion, and instead of disgrace you will rejoice in your inheritance. And so you will inherit a double portion in your land, and everlasting joy will be yours' (Isaiah 61:7 NIV).

I tried to take comfort in the thought that God would help us and that everlasting joy would be ours, even though our present situation seemed hopeless.

14

A SUMMER OF NEW BEGINNINGS

Saturday, 3 December 2016

Diary Entry

> After the results of the ultrasound scan, I calmed myself by remembering what was going right in my world. I'm really excited about being back in a school full-time. I am leaving this whole ovulation induction process behind and placing all my energy and time into being the best teacher I can be.

Monday, 5 December 2016

Diary Entry

> I opened up to the book of Ecclesiastes. 'Just as you can not understand the path of the wind or the mystery of a tiny baby growing in its mother's womb, so you cannot understand the activity of God who does all things' (Ecclesiastes 11:5 NLT).

After reading this, I realized that in this whole path of becoming a parent, trust was not one option for me; it was my only option.

Saturday, 10 December 2016

<u>Diary Entry</u>

> My period started yesterday. Rather than being devastated because this cycle did not work in the way we had hoped, I am filled with expectation, hope, and positivity about the future. God is perfect in all of His ways, and His timing is perfect.

> I am learning about humility. Whenever I face self-pity, my mind races back to the girls I met in Cape Town—the ones who lived in need or difficult situations, abandoned by those they loved, some of whom were struggling with depression or anxiety. The amazing thing was that they did not give up. They took each new day as it came. They fought to live another day. They chose to make better decisions. Thank you, God, for those incredible girls. Thank you that they inspire me to be the best I can be and not to take anything for granted.

Monday, 26 December 2016

<u>Diary Entry</u>

> God prompted me to put my disappointments, wants and desires aside this Christmas and make it fun and relaxing for others. Rather than focusing on what we don't have, we focused on what we do! Thankfully, with a better mindset, we all had a terrific time together.

Saturday, 31 December 2016

Diary Entry

> It's New Year's Eve. What will 2017 bring—more of the same, or something completely new? I sat and pondered this throughout the evening. Caught up in this doubtful train of thought, I could not muster the emotional strength to go out and join Ash at a NYE party we had been invited to. I'm sitting on our lounge room floor, face wet with tears, heart aching, and head filled with doubtful thoughts. What's wrong with me? Why am I being so self-absorbed? Why can't I get past this? Weary from sobbing, I rest my head on the carpet and sob a little more. God, I can't face this. This is too hard for me. Why won't you just answer me? Why can't we have a child— one that survives? What have I done wrong?

After penning these questions in my journal, I stared at the rest of the page. The tears streamed down my cheeks, and my whole head felt hot. I decided to wash my face. As I stared into the bathroom mirror, I wiped my nose with a piece of toilet paper and looked intently at my reflection. *What will I choose to believe? That God loves me and is listening to me? That He has a good plan for my life and that I need to trust and wait? Or will I believe that I am doomed to be childless, that God doesn't care about me, or that I don't deserve a child that lives past a day?*

Knowing God well from the past, and knowing how He had looked after me, I chose to believe His benevolence. As it was nearing midnight, I got dressed and prepared to join Ash at the party.

Thursday, 5 January 2017

<u>Diary Entry</u>

It's a new year! Before midnight on NYE, we watched the fireworks with some close friends at a local look out point. I was feeling a little upset because I thought that if Ash had married someone else, he might have children by now. I knew that he didn't think this way, but I was finding it difficult to overcome that thought.

On Monday evening, Ash and I spoke to close friends of ours about permanent care and adoption. Although I had agreed to try again with ovulation induction, I believed that having the perfect conditions for me to ovulate and conceive only one child could take years, so I continued to explore all my options.

Wednesday, 25 January 2017

<u>Diary Entry</u>

I woke up around 4.00 a.m. feeling dehydrated and restless. I may have had too much sodium yesterday. I took my last tablet to trigger my menstrual cycle yesterday. To be honest, I am only following the steps in the cycle because I gave my word that I would. I have no expectation beyond getting through this process and being able to get on with my job as a teacher.

Sunday, 29 January 2017

<u>Diary Entry</u>

This is the second day of my period. Ash and I discussed when we would try again, and he suggested that we wait until February, when things at school settle down. I agreed, as I have a few busy weeks of teaching coming up and I want to be at my best for my class. It does not really matter to me when we try, because I honestly doubt anything will come from it for a long time.

Wednesday, 1 February 2017

<u>Diary Entry</u>

Teaching and doing something that I enjoy is exhilarating! I was born for this. I adore my class and love working with these incredibly talented and intelligent staff members. I am truly blessed! I asked God to help me to do my very best.

Friday, 3 February 2017

<u>Diary Entry</u>

Ash and I attended a Bethel Worship evening at the Regent Theatre. It was amazing. I found myself grieving for Summer, Snow, and Sky again. On Sunday it will be their third birthday. I wept as God lovingly encouraged me. I whispered through tears as I sat down on the plush theatre seats surrounded by Ash and hundreds of other worshippers. I was grateful that the theatre was dark, as I needed privacy. The music, the lyrics, and the atmosphere lifted my spirit in a way that only praise and worship music could. In a moment of silence, I heard God whisper, 'You will have more children.' My tears flowed steadily again.

Sunday, 5 February 2017

<u>Diary Entry</u>

Three years old. Our boys Summer, Snow, and Sky were born three years ago. With each anniversary of their passing, it becomes easier to face as I remember back. The scars are still here, but the pain is gone.

Sunday, 26 February 2017

<u>Diary Entry</u>

Life has been busy with school assessments and lesson plans. Today would have been my grandmother's eightieth birthday. I thought about her a few times this week. What a blessing she was to me. I miss her so much. God, please help me to be just as much of a blessing to others in my life.

15

AUTUMN ARRIVALS

Thursday, 2 March 2017

<u>Diary Entry</u>

It is the second day of autumn, but the weather is still very warm. We are preparing to start the cycle soon. I am thoroughly enjoying teaching, so I am conflicted as to whether or not to go ahead.

However, I know that there is a very good chance that this may take a year or longer for me to produce only one viable follicle. It could take a while for my body to cooperate. I had several viable follicles, which was why we hadn't gone ahead during the last few cycles.

Sunday, 5 March 2017

<u>Diary Entry</u>

I had two FSH injections since Friday. Tonight I will have my third.

I carefully dialled the needle to the correct amount of FSH solution and pressed play on the music app on my phone. I had become accustomed to wearing comfortable clothing when I took injections, as it was easier to access the injection site when needed.

Tonight's choice of outfit was pyjamas. Having done this process many times, I was almost on automatic pilot. The injections didn't hurt any longer, and I tried to think of other things while I completed each step.

After clearing away all the medication, needles, and packaging, I organized the lounge room and prepared the snacks for our girls' night in. My mother, sister, and nieces arrived, and we watched a romantic comedy together. We chose a classic, which we had enjoyed together many times before. We all knew the iconic songs and could even recite the funny lines of the script. Feasting on pancakes, ice cream, snack food, and hot drinks, we bonded happily. I loved those evenings because they were refreshing to my soul.

Sunday, 12 March 2017

Diary Entry

> Ash and I are camping along the Murray River. We are in a remote spot. It's quiet, calm, and tranquil, except for the occasional flock of squawking cockatoos. Our caravan is parked on a risen part of the bank that overlooks the river. We are only about two metres away from the bank's edge. How lovely it is to be here. How beautiful this place is. The river looks like a smooth, glass plate; the morning sun reflecting on the water in the form of a long, straight beam is stunning.

Last night after dinner, Ash and I sat in silence, looking up at the large, bright moon. The moon's reflection rested on the river in protracted half-circular patterns. This has been the most relaxing camping trip ever even though I am on FSH injections. I took the last dose last night. Surprisingly, our doctor instructed us to have the booster tonight, and then Ash and I will try to get pregnant. I have two potential follicles. The other follicles are much smaller. Our doctor is happy for us to try to become pregnant with this cycle. The hormones are already affecting my body. I am actually shocked at how quickly this stage of the procedure has come. I was fully prepared to try all year and possibly become pregnant next year or the following year. Somehow my body has responded perfectly to the medication this time, and we are much further along than we expected to be.

Sunday, 19 March 2017

<u>Diary Entry</u>

Ash and my best friend organized for me to go to Adele's concert at Etihad Stadium as a birthday surprise. Wow! What a show, and what an incredible voice! My best friend and I had a fantastic night singing along to Adele's popular songs with the rest of the audience.

Tuesday, 21 March 2017

<u>Diary Entry</u>

My class planned a surprise party for me, and our school social committee organized a huge celebration for my birthday! One of my colleagues gave me a heart-warming speech, which brought me to tears.

Wow! What an incredible week of birthday celebrations. I feel treasured, loved, and cherished. My heart is full.

Monday, 27 March 2017

<u>Diary Entry</u>

This is the last week of the school term. This has been an intense but hugely rewarding term. I have learned and gained so much. My students are wonderful and caring, and the teachers and staff are like an extended family. However, I am looking forward to a rest in the school holidays. We are planning on going camping again. This time it will be in a caravan park with family.

Saturday, 1 April 2017

<u>Diary Entry</u>

This morning I felt a little strange. After asking God to help, I felt a God prompt to get a pregnancy test, so I decided to go to the local supermarket.

As I walked up to the checkout counter, I looked down in my basket and realized that the very thing I had come to the shops to purchase was not there. Many other items were nestled securely in the plastic shopping basket—just not the one I had sensed God tell me to get earlier this morning. *How could I have forgotten it?* I shrugged and walked back to the personal care aisle of the supermarket. Trying not to take too long, I selected the most economical choice and walked back to the same counter. The assistant behind the counter looked down at the test, back up at me, and then smiled briefly. After reciprocating the smile, I frowned and suddenly wished that I had chosen to use the self-serve checkout instead.

Sneaking back into the house, I tried to limit any noise, as Ash was sleeping after his overnight shift. Once I had unpacked the small load of groceries, I sat back on the couch in the lounge room, and it dawned on me how exhausted I suddenly felt. Placing the plastic bag containing the pregnancy test carefully on the coffee table, I sat back against the recliner. I tried to reason my way out of using it. The side effects I was experiencing were probably from the FSH injections. However, this morning I felt a little different. I couldn't explain it. I felt that it could be a cold or some other virus. That would account for the exhaustion, aches, and pains, but I also had sore breasts, and my face was warm and flushed. I couldn't eat much except for veggie chips. I had a few cramps and pains in my abdominal area but had not had my period yet. I was either pregnant or these physical symptoms could be due to extreme weariness after a taxing school term of teaching. In my usual habit of facing unpleasant or scary realities, I adopted the 'tearing off the Band-Aid' strategy and decided to do it quickly so that I could move ahead with my day.

Carefully placing the test on the ground on a piece of toilet paper, I stared at the plastic device until I saw the result. I was totally speechless. A rush of fear enveloped me, and I wondered whether the test could be faulty. 'If only I had bought the double test instead of one test packet,' I whispered to myself. Unsure what to do, I left the bathroom and placed the used test back on the bathroom floor.

Desperately examining the glossy pamphlet of instructions, I whispered each and every word again as I paced back and forth in the living room. My conclusion was that this company guaranteed only 99 per cent accuracy, so I could be in the 1 per cent. After a few moments of frantic contemplation, I decided that I could not hold this heavy burden by myself, so I took a photo of the test result and sent it to Ash. Not sure that he would respond, as

I knew he might not be woken by the text message, I walked into the bedroom. After trying to wake him up gently,

I explained that I had taken a pregnancy test. Ash, still groggy with sleep, peered down at the picture of the pregnancy test on my phone and chuckled lightly, and then after a few minutes of chatting, he rolled over and placed his head back on the pillow. That was it. I was expecting him to be as surprised as I was, but instead all he managed was this nonchalant response. Later that day, after he had woken up again, we discussed the validity of pregnancy tests, and Ash assured me that those tests were very accurate. However, I was determined to get a blood test with my GP as soon as I possibly could.

<u>Diary Entry</u>

Thinking back over my week, I remember being a little queasy whilst sitting next to someone who I believe forgot to put deodorant on. I was extremely tired after school yesterday. I've noticed that I have been taking things to heart, or being sensitive, moody, agitated, upset, and very tired! Those are all signs of early pregnancy. Even though we hoped for this pregnancy, I'm now stunned that it is real!

However, it is April Fool's Day, so anything is possible.

Sunday, 2 April 2017

<u>Diary Entry</u>

I'm still stunned by this incredible miracle. Thank you, God! There is a real possibility that Ash and I are going to have another child, just as you said we would! *Amazing!*

Ash reminded me that the test was 99 per cent accurate, so he was in no rush for me to get a blood test. I will email our fertility nurse tomorrow. I thought back over this past week and realized that I was having symptoms that line up with an increase of progesterone in my body. There is a slight chance that we could have twins, as there were two large follicles. God, I trust you with everything to do with this pregnancy.

If I am correct in my calculations, I am already in week four of my pregnancy. This means that we can have a scan in four weeks' time. Then we can tell everyone after twelve weeks. Ash wants to do a big announcement to our family and friends, which will be in the second-to-last week of May.

Ash and I have already talked about possible baby names.

Monday, 3 April 2017

<u>Diary Entry</u>

I emailed my fertility nurse. She was very excited but reminded me to stay grounded until the blood test results were confirmed. I told Ash, but he is confident that I am pregnant. I feel ill when I think about having hot drinks, and I am unable to eat potato crisps, which is usually my favourite snack. We had a blood test at a pathology clinic. Ash has been incredibly supportive. In the church service yesterday, I heard God tell me again, 'You are pregnant.'

I think that I find it hard to hold on to hope because I'm more afraid of disappointment. Ash reminded me to hold this with an open hand, which means to trust God and release control to Him.

Wednesday, 5 April 2017

<u>Diary Entry</u>

I got a call from our fertility nurse to say that the blood test results confirm that I am pregnant!

After ending our phone conversation, I prayed and committed this entire pregnancy to Him. God, I ask for your protection, provision, and wisdom. I will tell anyone who will hear about your goodness and the miracle you have given us.

Friday, 7 April 2017

<u>Diary Entry</u>

It's the end of the first week of the school holidays. I've taken every opportunity to relax this week. Last week at this time, I didn't even know that I was pregnant. Yesterday I was five weeks pregnant! In two weeks' time, I am going in for my first scan.

Saturday, 8 April 2017

<u>Diary Entry</u>

I woke up and found dark red discharge. I had a little trouble sleeping last night because I felt nauseated throughout the night. My heart is weighed down with worry. God, please help me!

Saturday, 15 April 2017

<u>Diary Entry</u>

We had a great time camping and even stayed an extra night. I've been having more discharge, but my fertility nurse said that 30 per cent of women have this and are fine. I have been feeling very ill. Our fertility nurse said that my pregnancy hormones are very high, so I may be pregnant with multiples again. God, you said that I have nothing to worry about, so I will trust you. I've been feeling very lethargic and tired. I'm finding it hard to be motivated to do anything these days.

Tuesday, 18 April 2017

<u>Diary Entry</u>

I felt really ill yesterday, so I stayed home from work. Each time I tried to move around, I thought I was going to be sick. My emotions are also peaking. I spent most of the day sleeping because I did not feel the nausea while I slept. Even journaling makes me nauseated. This is all I can manage to write for now.

Wednesday, 19 April 2017

<u>Diary Entry</u>

Stayed home again today. Visited our GP yesterday, and she suggested that I stay home. She gave me a prescription for an anti-nausea medication. Our GP journeyed with us during our last pregnancy and wants me to be very cautious this time.

I slept most of the day. I am hoping to go to work tomorrow. Ash and I are planning on speaking to my school leaders and bosses about the possibility of me working part-time. On my doctor's advice, I need to make sure that I am resting as much as possible.

The most exciting news is that I had a scan and found out that we are pregnant with *twins!*

Saturday, 22 April 2017

I went to work on Thursday even though I was feeling grey. I took some medication to help with nausea. Some of my colleagues could detect that something was different with me. It was very hard to hide. I spoke to my team leader and supervisors. They were all very supportive. My students seemed concerned about my health and showed great care and affection. They are such amazing children. I am blessed to be their teacher. The plan that we discussed was the idea of me going part-time. There is a very capable teacher who is able to teach the class during my days off. My doctor had advised that I still needed a lot of rest. One of my students spent a long time making a special picture for me on the computer. I was touched beyond words.

My sense of smell has increased. I was sure that my superpower was my ability to smell everything everywhere. I was learning to eat small meals regularly and to drink more water. My memory is not as sharp as it used to be. I am moving a lot slower than I used to, mainly because of exhaustion and trying to avoid feeling sick. I am sitting around and lying down a lot, like a sloth. I sleep as much as I can. Ash has been wonderful in taking care of the housework and looking after me. He has been cleaning, tidying, sorting, managing, and cooking! What an incredible man! As I drifted off to sleep, I imagined Ash and myself on stage at church at our children's baby dedication, acknowledging God for His faithfulness and thanking our family and friends for their support. We have begun the mission of telling everyone in our world about our two precious gifts from God. On Wednesday we went for another ultrasound scan. Ash and I saw two beautiful children—fraternal twins. We heard and saw their hearts beating. They are both healthy. We have our first photo of our children—a sonogram.

Thursday, 4 May 2017

Diary Entry

> I'm still experiencing pregnancy symptoms especially nausea if I don't eat. I feel tired and bloated, and I am unable to eat sugar, potato crisps, or anything greasy or oily. In fact, the mere thought of these foods makes my stomach churn.

The past few weeks have been harrowing. I was sick and unable to go to school. I briefly went on Wednesday but felt ill, threw up, and was overwhelmed by worry and nausea. I couldn't keep still or calm myself down. As I entered the classroom, I quickly turned the heating down because it was like a furnace. Waves of nausea washed over me every few minutes. All I wanted to do was put my head on the desk and sleep. I pushed through what I was feeling and set up the room for the day, but then, as the ill feeling continued, I walked to the main office, briefly greeted some staff members, and then walked straight to the bathroom. I was overcome with nausea and emotion. I felt better for a moment after throwing up, but then it all returned. As I emerged from the bathroom, two staff members came to my aid, but all I could do was cry.

After another trip to the bathroom, I sat down in the staff room for a while. I called Ash, and he arranged for a friend to pick me up from school. My friend helped me to find my place to rest and even did some chores before leaving me to sleep. She returned that afternoon with snacks and helped with picking up my car from the school. I slept until late into the evening. A few hours later, I woke and had a small snack and a few sips of water, and I then returned to bed. I was awake when Ash arrived home from work that night. We chatted briefly. I hadn't realized how much this ordeal affected me. We discussed the possibility of having a replacement teacher until the morning sickness passed. I was still exhausted and fell back to sleep.

I woke up early the next day, had a warm cup of milk and honey, had a pregnancy vitamin, and went back to bed. I tried to delay taking the anti-nausea medication, but that lasted only a few hours. Ash had reassured me that I didn't need to worry about disappointing everyone at school if I was unable to work. I was also worrying about our finances if I stayed home. After talking to him about my concerns, I was relieved and was able to relax and rest.

Saturday, 6 May 2017

Diary Entry

> Ash and I went into school to discuss our final decision with regard to my work. I was very sad to be leaving my workplace but relieved that I would be able to rest and not have to stress any more.
>
> God, please help me to focus solely on looking after these precious babies you have entrusted to us.

Tuesday, 9 May 2017

<u>Diary Entry</u>

We visited our GP again today. I felt ill in the waiting room as the smells in the air caused my nausea to arise. Our GP was helpful and kind and tried to make me feel as comfortable as possible. I have been experiencing crazy dreams that made no sense at all. On average, I would have about four dreams per night and a few extras during the day. I guess I was sleeping a lot, so the chances of dreaming were much higher than in the past. I had been taking anti-nausea medication every day. I have been losing weight rapidly. I was struggling to keep food down but forced myself to drink water as often as possible. Our GP advised that if I was unable to keep liquid and food in my stomach, I might need to go on a drip in the emergency section of the hospital. God, please help my body to cooperate so I won't have to go on a drip.

It is two weeks until I will be in my second trimester. My belly is growing, my hair is greasy, I have sore breasts, I am tired all of the time, I am nauseated by smells, I can't eat much, I am not a fan of water, and I have a very dry forehead, bad breath, stronger nails, and weird gums, but it's all worth it!

I placed my keys in my handbag and lowered the handbag down onto the couch, as I felt the need to visit the lavatory. This was a frequent activity in my day and or night. During my visit to the toilet, I noticed that I had a bleed. As if a bolt of lightning hit me right there in the cubicle, I sat stunned. I thought that I was losing the babies. Panic set in. My mouth dried up, but I cried out to God. The air in the room seemed to have been sucked out, and I began to panic. I dashed out of the bathroom to find my handbag, pulled out my phone, and called Ash. I explained what

I was experiencing. He told me to remain calm and to trust God. He also encouraged me to call the doctor.

Motionless on our bed, I waited for the doctor to return my call. All I could do was pray silently. Every muscle in my body was tense. These sensations reminded me of the moment when I was about to give birth to the triplets. I desperately tried to calm myself by speaking out the promises that I had in my heart from God. I began to recite the many verses I looked to for strength. Meditating on these scriptures, I began to cry, but tears were not going to help me, so I did what I knew would be good no matter the outcome—I sang a song of praise to God. I lifted up words about His goodness, His faithfulness, and His love. I thanked Him for not leaving me and told Him that I would be a happy mother of children. As I sang and spoke to God, I sensed I had entered a cocoon of protection. I was safe because He was near.

As I was caught up in this incredible atmosphere, my phone rang. It was my fertility doctor. She reassured me that bleeding in early pregnancy could be quite normal. She recommended that I have an ultrasound to set my mind at ease. Ash drove straight home after my phone call. After a while, my bleeding stopped and I sat on the couch wondering whether this was where our journey with our twins ended. Despite my awe-inspiring encounter with God in our bathroom, I fell into a hole of doubt.

Diary Entry

> I don't think I can do this again, God. Please don't take them away from us. I allowed the tears to fall as I wrote these words.

Ash was kind and extremely attentive. He suggested that we watch a film together. It was a heart-warming comedy and gave me a much-needed break from my thoughts. As I walked towards the bedroom, Ash reassured me and told me that he was confident that this was normal. I decided to defer to his confidence in this, as I had none of my own. As I rested on my own in the bedroom, I heard a gentle God whisper, 'You have nothing to worry about. They will make it to the end.'

Those words brought comfort and hovered over me as I drifted off to sleep.

Friday, 12 May 2017

<u>Diary Entry</u>

> The bleeding has stopped. Thank you, God! My sister dropped in some delicious dinner. I hope I will be able to eat it.

Thursday, 18 May 2017

<u>Diary Entry</u>

> I totally missed yesterday. I woke up this morning thinking that it was Wednesday, not sure how that happened. My belly is still growing. Pregnancy is a fascinating experience.

> My family and friends have been wonderful in visiting and supporting us. In two days, I will be twelve weeks pregnant! I am excited that all is going well with our little babies!

Sunday, 21 May 2017

<u>Diary Entry</u>

> Tomorrow it will be twelve weeks. That means my first
> trimester is done! With each week, my confidence grows
> that our babies will survive. However, I am careful not to
> become too relaxed about it. God, please help me.

Thursday, 25 May 2017

<u>Diary Entry</u>

> We went for our twelve-week scan today. There seems to
> be a problem with one of our twins.

Frozen in time, I sat on the examining table, and my heart sank
as the words come out of the doctor's mouth. He explained that
there might be a problem with the health of one of our twins.
Among the outcomes could be heart problems or a genetic issue,
such as Down's syndrome. He looked sympathetic as he relayed
the unpleasant news.

I instantly began to tear up.

The doctor may have sensed that Ash and I needed some time
to process this information, because moments later he excused
himself and left the room. I burst out crying. *How could this be?*
I thought as I swallowed down the ache in my throat. My whole
face was hot, flushed. My eyes were streaming with tears, and I
nearly allowed myself to begin to sob. Ash tried his best to comfort
me, but I just sat there in a mess. A few minutes later the doctor
reappeared and began explaining the possible issues in further
detail.

Diary Entry

> As the doctor continued talking, I felt as if I were in a dream—no, a nightmare! *Are you serious?* I thought to myself as his words streamed out. I kept eye contact with him, but my mind was far away.

Firstly I felt scared, then angry, and then sad. Then I had the thought, *What if our child does have a genetic challenge like Down's syndrome and is unable to cope on his or her own? Who will be there to take care of him or her when Ash and I die? My heart is broken, our poor little baby. Why has this child's life been affected in this way? Will our other child feel guilty for being healthy? How will we cope?* This is assuming that both babies survive this pregnancy. God, I have nothing left in my faith tank. If you don't help us, I don't know what we'll do! I can't stop crying. I feel like this is unfair. *Why can others have perfectly healthy babies and yet we struggle?*

On the way home in the car, I heard God. 'You are being tested. This is a test. How will your rise?'

I answered quietly. 'I can't rise. I'm just going to sit here in the dust of this disappointment.'

I sobbed for a while on the couch in our lounge room, deflated and still a little angry that this had been allowed to happen. Our one consolation was that we still had both twins and there was hope that they would survive the entire pregnancy. Ash and I chatted for a while, and he encouraged me by telling me that I have a choice to trust God or to remain angry.

I had a restless night's sleep.

Friday, 26 May 2017

<u>Diary Entry</u>

> Yesterday was tough for Ash and me, like an unexpected
> punch in the stomach. I let a few of our family and friends
> know and asked them to pray with us. Last night when
> Ash got home, we chatted about where we were at with
> this news. I shared the thoughts and verses that helped
> me through the day.

As my pen hovered over my page in my journal, I decided to go to
my source of strength and hope. I opened up to Psalm 121 in the
Bible: 'I lift my eyes to the mountains-where does my help come
from? My help comes from the Lord, the Maker of heaven and
earth' (Psalm 121:1–2 NIV).

The best result we could hope and pray for was that both babies
would be born at the right time, completely healthy. I know that
there are other people in the world who are hurting over issues
that are so much worse than ours: tragedies that we cannot even
imagine, relationships that are broken, lost family members,
terminal illness, addictions, and abuse.

Sunday, 28 May 2017

<u>Diary Entry</u>

> I read part of Queen Esther's story in the Bible (Esther
> chapters 1–10 in the NIV). She showed great courage.
> God, please help me to show great courage with our
> health news.

Monday, 29 May 2017

<u>Diary Entry</u>

> We are in week thirteen of our pregnancy! I am coping much better in the mornings but still quite unwell in the evenings. I am tired, but I still have some energy to get me through my day. Early this morning, I felt a twitch in my belly; I assumed it was a growth twitch. I asked God to please bring complete restoration to our baby's body.

My grandfather visited us today with some homemade mince curry pastries.

The hospital we are registered with called to confirm our appointment for an ultrasound next Tuesday. The previous day, I swore that I experienced a flutter from the left side of my belly, which actually woke me up.

Twin ultrasound appointment.

16

WINTER WARNINGS

Sunday, 4 June 2017

<u>Diary Entry</u>

My life is filled with news both light and shade. As I sat resting with God's thoughts infusing mine, I sensed that all would be well with our twins.

Wednesday, 7th June 2017

<u>Diary Entry</u>

Ash and I had our ultrasound appointment at the hospital today. The doctors and nurses were kind and helpful. We were in the ultrasound room for two hours. Two doctors consulted about our twin on the left. Our babies look so cute. They both covered their faces and hid while the sonographer was trying to calculate their measurements. The babies had their feet positioned on my bladder and moved a lot during the ultrasound, which made it pretty uncomfortable for me. Their little feet and hands are so adorable. Thank you, God, for allowing us to see them. Thank you God, that you created them, are forming them, and will continue to form them in my womb. Please protect them and keep them safe as you promise.

Tuesday, 13 June 2017

Diary Entry

My best friend is engaged! I am so excited! Her fiancé took her to the top of a hill at sunset to propose. So romantic! She and I chatted for a while on the phone. It was wonderful! The wedding is planned for late October of this year. I will be heavily pregnant by then, I hope.

Wednesday, 14 June 2017

Diary Entry

Ash and I watched the Golden State Warriors beat the Cavaliers in the NBA finals! I was sure that I felt our little ones move in my belly. Maybe they enjoy hearing the basketball game. I am feeling so much better these days. Although I am very tired, sometimes I don't feel queasy until much later in the day.

Monday, 19 June 2017

Diary Entry

Sixteen weeks today! Thank you, God. I am almost 100 per cent sure that I can feel our little twinsies moving in my belly, especially when I am still for a long time.

Tuesday, 20 June 2017

<u>Diary Entry</u>

My best friend came over in the evening and gifted us with two gorgeous baby suits that she bought during her time in the USA. She showed me her beautiful engagement ring and asked me whether I would do a speech at her wedding. I was amazed, as it was exactly what I saw years ago in my dream—that I would be standing at her bridal table, dressed up and giving a speech. In the dream, I had a pregnant belly.

Sunday, 25 June 2017

<u>Diary Entry</u>

A few of our close friends offered us their white/cream-coloured couch. We had been looking to buy a bigger couch, so we accepted gratefully.

Friday, 30 June 2017

<u>Diary Entry</u>

Ash and I went to our ultrasound appointment at the hospital and found out that we are having *two boys!* The baby's measurements were all correct. They appear to be developing well. The doctor said that their size was good, if not slightly larger than average. There still may be issues with one of the twins, which could mean that he has developmental problems. Both babies' heart functions were good, which was a positive sign. Even though the possibility of health issues for one baby hung over us, we were overjoyed to see them on the ultrasound scan.

Five boys! God has given us five boys—three in heaven and two in my belly. We are totally thrilled!

We have another scan in four weeks' time. I will be passing on any girls' toys and clothing to parents of baby girls. Knowing their gender helps us to plan. We already have a few neutral-coloured outfits for our boys. Ash and I went to Chadstone Shopping Centre on the way home from the hospital and bought our boys two grey jumpers with blue bicycle prints, and blue puffy vests.

Ash and I have been working on some name selections for our twins—possibly Zed and Jay?

Amazingly, I have been walking ten to twelve minutes each day around our neighbourhood, and I am already feeling the benefits of regular exercise.

Monday, 3 July 2017

Diary Entry

I am eighteen weeks pregnant today! This is around the same time I started to have trouble with the triplets. This thought did cross my mind several times, but I will trust God. I am looking forward to starting back at Sisterhood at our church. God, please help me to be a blessing to others.

Saturday, 8 July 2017

Diary Entry

Baby Zed and Baby Jay have been moving around a lot in my tummy. God, please continue to protect them, strengthen them, and bless them as they grow to full term. I pray for our boys every day.

Sunday, 9 July 2017

<u>Diary Entry</u>

I went to our church service in the morning with Ash. Our boys loved the praise and worship part of the service; they moved around a lot as the music played.

Monday, 10 July 2017

<u>Diary Entry</u>

I am nineteen weeks pregnant today! My best friend's wedding is in fifteen to sixteen weeks' time. Ash would like to announce our pregnancy on Facebook at six months (which is in five weeks' time). I would like to delay the announcement for as long as possible.

Monday, 17 July 2017

<u>Diary Entry</u>

I had a catch-up with my best friend yesterday. She showed me a picture of her wearing her wedding dress. I became so worked up, overcome with emotions, and excited that I got a bloody nose!

I am twenty weeks pregnant! I was reluctant to do anything public about my pregnancy, because I was scared. However, God has given me two promises about this pregnancy that I choose to hold on to.

Ash and I went to a huge baby store on Saturday but were so overwhelmed with all the products, goods, and items that we ended up sitting in feeding chairs for a while and then left without buying a single thing. We have another appointment at the hospital today.

Saturday, 22 July 2017

<u>Diary Entry</u>

Ash and I watched an episode of *Insight* about twins. We have been organizing our nursery. Our boys have been moving a lot throughout the show. Rightie started, and Leftie continued. I'm not sure which one is Zed and which one is Jay.

Saturday, 29 July 2017

<u>Diary Entry</u>

Thank you, God, for an encouraging report from the doctor at the hospital after another ultrasound. The boys are roughly the same size. Leftie might be slightly smaller, but not by much. Both boys were very active during the ultrasound session. The doctor was so pleased with how our boys are growing that we won't need to go back to the Foetal Development Unit again but will now be monitored by the Twins Clinic in hospital. They have given us the option of having other tests to find out whether our baby has a genetic issue.

Ash and I discussed it, and as there is a small chance that I could miscarry as a result of the testing, we have decided not to go ahead with any further genetic testing. We choose to trust God for two healthy boys.

During the ultrasound, we got the thumbs up from Rightie, and Leftie covered his face again when they tried to measure his nose. He also turned his back on us completely. They are the cutest kids! They are already showing signs of having their father's sense of humour.

Tuesday, 1 August 2017

<u>Diary Entry</u>

We went to our first appointment in the Twins Clinic at the hospital.

This was the same hospital where we lost our triplets. I became emotional just thinking about it, as the fear started to creep into my thoughts. I had to fight hard to regain control of my mind and used every ounce of energy to fight off the urge to give in to fear.

Our appointment with the new doctor just made it worse, as she jumped into all the things that could possibly go wrong with pregnancy and then surprised me by asking questions about our experience with our triplets. Unprepared for any of that, I didn't react well and I struggled to remain calm. I was grateful that Ash was in the room to support me. We also had to book an appointment at the Pregnancy Assessment Unit, where I last visited the day we lost our triplets. All of this just felt overwhelming. I felt as if a cloud of doubt settled over me as I left the appointment.

<u>Diary Entry</u>

Later that day, as I sat on my bed, I realized that I am twenty-two weeks pregnant and have made it further than with the triplets. Thank you, God.

I read a verse from the Bible: 'But my eyes are fixed on you Sovereign Lord, in you I take refuge' (Psalm 141:8 NIV).

Wednesday, 2 August 2017

Diary Entry

> I booked our pregnancy workshops at the hospital for 21 October. It will be a full day, which may be tiring, but Ash will be with me, so I'm sure I will be fine. I am thinking about the possibility of having a baby shower.

In the past, attending a baby shower was not on the top of my list. To be honest, some of the baby showers were more unpleasant than others, as people found this the perfect opportunity to joke about or pry into why Ash and I did not have children. The words did not seem to bother me before Ash and I lost our triplets, but they cut deep after the possibility of parenthood seemed almost unattainable to us. Most people were kind and considerate when it came to talking about this topic, but there were the occasional conversations that made me cry.

Friday, 4 August 2017

Diary Entry

> I had a chat with my best friend's mother for a while. She is a woman of amazing faith! I admire her and thank God for her. She prayed for me years ago at one of my birthday parties, asking that God would give us children. As she has seven children of her own, I believe that she is well qualified to believe that for us. She reminded me that God divinely creates each child and makes no mistakes. I was incredibly encouraged by her honesty, faith, and example.

Friday, 11 August 2017

<u>Diary Entry</u>

Looking at our calendar, I see we still have a little while left until the possible arrival of our twins. In thirteen weeks' time, we will hopefully say hello to our boys face-to-face. God, I ask that our boys be born at your appointed time. We are hoping to announce the good news at six months.

Ash wants to post the news of our boys on Facebook and Instagram. He sees it as a good-news story, which will be a great encouragement to people. I was waiting until the six-month mark, but Ash would like to do it on Monday, when I am twenty-four weeks pregnant. I think that I am still holding back in fear, so I will agree to go along with his plan instead.

Monday, 14 August 2017

<u>Diary Entry</u>

I am twenty-four weeks pregnant! Thank you, God! It is ten weeks until my best friend's wedding! In the mornings, after I muster the strength to lift myself out of bed, I enjoy a breakfast of toast and water, and then make a list of things I can do for that day.

Monday, 21 August 2017

<u>Diary Entry</u>

I am twenty-five weeks pregnant! It's only nine weeks until my best friend and her fiancé get married.

The boys were both very active in my belly this morning between three and five. The song 'Radio' from my album *Finding Me* has been played on the radio station LightFM. I play the song throughout the day, and the boys seem to move more when it is playing.

Friday, 25 August 2017

<u>Diary Entry</u>

We had a great catch-up with a friend of mine who had her own set of twins. She is a generous and caring mentor to me. We talked about my pregnancy, and she shared her wisdom about having twins. It was an enjoyable afternoon, and I am grateful for her friendship. Being at home is certainly creating a place where family and friends are able to drop in and spend time with me. Ash and I watched the film *What to Expect When You're Expecting.*

Sunday, 27 August 2017

<u>Diary Entry</u>

Ash and I posted the announcement of the twins on Facebook. People have been incredibly kind with their comments and well wishes. Thank you, God, for the opportunity to share this good news!

17

FLOURISHING IN SPRING

Saturday, 2 September 2017

<u>Diary Entry</u>

> Spring has sprung. Ash and I went for another scan at
> the hospital. The doctor was happy with both babies'
> measurements. This doctor's demeanour was warm,
> caring, and positive. Later that afternoon, we had our
> appointment with our Twins Clinic doctor. I also have
> an appointment for my glucose test.

Reclining on the padded chair in the waiting room of the clinic, I
smiled at the other people across the corridor from me. All of the
ladies in this clinic were obviously pregnant. My name was called
a few moments later, so I waddled across to the examining room.

Greeted by a cheerful nurse at the door, I instantly felt relaxed.
She invited me to take a seat and asked me a series of questions
to confirm my identity, and she then proceeded to explain the
process. The nurse handed me a bottle of the glucose solution,
which I consumed in less than two minutes. It was not the most
pleasant two minutes of my life, but I endured it and thankfully
made it all the way to the end of the container.

As I walked out of the room, I prayed that I would not throw up, because I knew that I would have to start the whole process from the beginning if I did.

Fully prepared for this procedure, I decided to bring one of the parenting books I had received from a family member. Once seated again, I set my alarm on my phone carefully so that even if the nurses were busy, I could alert them of the time for my next blood test. Patients came and went, and I felt only slightly ill about twenty minutes into my waiting period.

The clinic was buzzing with life, so my first hour flew past. I briefly saw an old friend who was also pregnant with a boy. We chatted for a while, and then she had to leave for her appointment with her obstetrician.

The next hour seemed to drag on, as I was one of the last patients in the waiting room. I remembered having this test with the triplets, and it caused terrible feeling. Ash was with me for that test, and I remember that I had to be taken into a consulting room to lie down on a bed until it passed. Fortunately I did not throw up during that test three years ago. Now I prayed that God would help me to push through the discomfort of this glucose test. Having been unable to eat breakfast this morning because this was a blood sugar test, I felt hungry and nauseated. Seconds away from alerting a nurse, I decided to walk to the bathroom. Standing up and moving around helped, and I instantly felt better when I returned to the waiting room.

The second last patient left, so I was on my own. The nurses came out of their consulting room and chatted with me as we waited. My last blood test completed, I walked out of the clinic satisfied and grateful that I had been able to get through the entire procedure without becoming ill. Walking back to my car whilst munching on some snacks, I reflected on how different this experience was to my last glucose test. I had a hopeful sense that this pregnancy was going to have a different ending.

Friday, 8 September 2017

<u>Diary Entry</u>

> I had a restless night because my feet are swelling. I weighed myself, and I can't believe that I have gained 900 grams in two weeks. I have been advised that I can gain only another six kilos and remain in a healthy weight range. I called the Twins Clinic to find out my results from the glucose test. I was thrilled to find out that I do not have gestational diabetes. However, I do have an iron and vitamin D deficiency, so I need to take supplements as soon as possible.

My brother-in-law very kindly offered to paint a chest of drawers for the nursery—one that Ash used in his bedroom years ago.

Monday, 11 September 2017

<u>Diary Entry</u>

> I am twenty-eight weeks pregnant! That's six months! Thank you, God!

> I am noticing that I am quite tired these days and need frequent rest breaks. I sleep in most mornings. I attended a good friend's baby shower and connected with a few friends that I have not seen in a while. It was a great time of celebrating with my friends. It was fun taking a back-to-back profile photo of our baby bellies together.

Monday, 18 September 2017

Diary Entry

We had a wonderful time with our family and friends, celebrating my grandfather's eightieth birthday. I enjoyed socializing, but I was exhausted by the end of the night!

Our appointment at the clinic went surprisingly well. The doctor was positive, and we even joked around with her.

I am twenty-nine weeks pregnant. However, my pregnant belly measured at thirty-four weeks, which is equivalent to a singleton baby. My blood pressure was normal, and the babies' heartbeats were normal. The doctor examined me and said that they were both facing down. She even giggled and said that they have hard bottoms. We discussed the Twins Talk event happening at the hospital and the parenting class. I left the appointment feeling hopeful. Our next appointment is an ultrasound on Monday.

Saturday, 23 September 2017

Diary Entry

My wonderful family and friends organized a fantastic baby shower for us! The food was plentiful, the conversations flowed, and the atmosphere was warm and welcoming. Some of us stayed at my aunt and uncle's house for dinner and then cleaned up and went home. Ash and I went to bed and then woke up a few hours later because we were excited about opening the baby shower presents. Everyone showered us with extraordinarily generous gifts! Our boys are very blessed!

Monday, 25 September 2017

Diary Entry

We went to our ultrasound appointment at the hospital. The baby's measurements are all good! Relieved that all is well with the health of our boys so far, I said a prayer of thanks to God.

Saturday, 30 September 2017

Diary Entry

It is my best friend's bridal shower today. I am a little nervous about the big day ahead. I hope that I will have enough energy to last through all the celebrations.

I think that I was energized by the excitement of the day. We had a terrific time celebrating! The Richmond Tigers won the AFL Grand Final. Ash was thrilled!

I can't believe that I am thirty-one weeks pregnant! The boys moved first thing in the morning, and then in the afternoon, when I was resting. They also move after I attend the lavatory, which happens frequently, so basically the babies move nearly all the time! I have done some reading about their development. According to the website about baby growth, their senses have developed now, their brain activity is increasing, and their eyes are responding to light.

Ash has done an incredible job organizing the house so that we will be ready for the twins' arrival!

Wednesday, 4 October 2017

<u>Diary Entry</u>

> The boys' movements are becoming more and more prominent. My dress arrived for my best friend's wedding. I really hope it fits.

Saturday, 7 October 2017

<u>Diary Entry</u>

> Ash and I went to the Pregnancy, Babies and Children Expo. We organized to meet a friend of ours, who helped us with making good choices in regard to care products for the twins. He and his wife had twins years ago, and he shared some of their challenges and joys. It was a rewarding experience, and we are grateful to him for his support and help in every way. I hope one day Ash and I will be able to be a blessing to others who are about to have twins.

> Excited but tired, we entered the huge warehouse of stalls. I found myself waddling and needing regular rest breaks these days, so I was always on the lookout for bathroom signs and benches. We searched the map for the stall we had come to see, and Ash carefully plotted our route. The peculiar feeling of being part of some sort of 'large belly club' came over me as we walked past many pregnant women down the aisles of the expo. It was as if I were engaged in a strange pregnancy parade as I walked up and down the pathways, watching women's various belly and breast sizes and interesting styles of maternity clothing. We found our friend's stall and enjoyed a great conversation about the fun and flaws of parenthood. He shared his insights on parenting twins and generously helped us with the products we needed.

We were hoping to get the nursery set up and organized in the next two weeks. I experienced pressure in my lower abdomen a few times this week and have been feeling tightening once a day.

We had another appointment at the hospital. We will see the doctor in three weeks and have our last scan. Rightie's heartbeat is faster than Leftie's. My belly measured at thirty-nine weeks, close to full term for a singleton, even though I am only thirty-two weeks pregnant!

We are hoping to make it to thirty-six weeks, which is only four weeks away.

Saturday, 21 October 2017

<u>Diary Entry</u>

Ash and I attended a parenting course at the hospital. I was having trouble getting out of bed, so we went after the first session. It was a good time of absorbing new information and meeting other expectant parents. Ash did a great job with wrapping the baby, and I took photographs of the copious notes, charts, and lists that were presented. The course facilitator was relaxed and personable. I'm really glad we attended.

Sunday, 22 October 2017

<u>Diary Entry</u>

I have decided to try to sleep this discomfort off. I have been in contact with Ash, and he said that he would support me in whatever decision I made. I am resting on our bed with my Bible and journal.

For the last few hours, I have been getting lower abdominal cramps. They are not painful, but uncomfortable. I called Ash at work and then the Pregnancy Assessment Unit at the hospital, as I noticed some drastic changes. I started timing my cramps around seven-thirty this evening, but they have been inconsistent.

The midwife from the hospital told me to call back in an hour, but I may need to go into hospital to be checked. This conversation took me back to when I went into preterm labour with the triplets. My whole body tightened with anxiety. The midwife mentioned that these kinds of irregular contractions could go on for days or even weeks, so I should not be alarmed unless I notice other indicators.

Diary Entry

It's been an hour, and I called the Pregnancy Assessment Unit again and spoke to another midwife because I started to notice my back pain increasing, my belly tightening, and the cramping feeling becoming more consistent. I'm not too concerned, as it just feels like bad period pain, nothing more. I am timing the belly tightening, but it is still irregular, so I'm ruling out labour pains. I am trying to remain relaxed by journaling.

It's eleven p.m. Ash and I have decided that he should come home to take me to the hospital to be assessed. Amazingly he was able to find someone to replace him at work. We'll drive to the hospital together. I am exhausted, but I am still experiencing the contractions.

God please help us. Please protect our little ones!

Once Ash and I drove into the hospital car park, he wheeled me to the Pregnancy Assessment Unit, where the midwife that I had previously spoken to on the phone helped us. They tried to monitor the boys' hearts. It was a difficult time for me, as I was sitting on the same chair that I sat on when I went into preterm labour with the triplets three years before. A doctor came down from the operating theatre to help. After a while of monitoring the boys' heartbeats and taking other measurements, they wheeled me into the birthing suite, as it was difficult to monitor two babies' heartbeats in that location. In the birthing suite, the doctor asked for permission to give me an internal examination. I agreed, and he announced that I had dilated seven centimetres and that our boys were going to be born soon. All the medical staff began preparing for their birth. The room suddenly filled with people, and I was given an epidural.

I was completely shocked at this sudden turn of events especially since a few hours earlier I did not even think that I was having contractions. I was quite unprepared and even told Ash that I couldn't go through with the labour as I was concerned about missing my best friend's wedding on Thursday! Ash calmed me and encouraged me to cooperate with the medical staff because we were about to meet our babies.

The doctors in charge were awesome; so were the midwives and, of course, my amazing husband. Everyone clicked into place like they were all part of a well-oiled machine. At times there were at least twelve people in the room—a huge contrast to the one or two midwives in the room down the hallway, where we lost the triplets. Overwhelmed, I started to cry, as I was afraid that it was too soon for the twins to be born. The doctor reassured me that thirty-four weeks was not too early. Ash was a true superstar and rose to every challenge of the occasion. He helped the medical staff and was a constant comfort and encourager to me through the whole process.

It was such a surreal feeling when Zed started to cry and they placed him on my chest. What a beautiful boy! He was then moved to his intensive care cot so they could help him with respiration. Jay was not far behind—twenty-seven minutes, to be exact. He, too, was placed on my chest. I was overwhelmed with joy. He was so gorgeous! He, too, was put in an intensive care cot, and both boys were taken into the NICU of the hospital.

Once our miracle babies had been delivered, everyone began packing up; and after further procedures, I was moved to a ward in hospital to recover. The withdrawal from the epidural was most unpleasant, but I was grateful that both boys had been born safely.

I was absolutely wiped out. Ash stayed with the boys as I slept for six hours without stirring. After I woke up, Ash took me to visit Zed and Jay. I cannot accurately describe the way my heart felt when I looked at those two precious children. It felt as if I were dreaming. Looking at them in their cots in NICU with tubes and pipes all around them was difficult, but they were alive. We thanked God for being with us through the whole delivery process, and we prayed over both Zed and Jay.

Diary Entry

> I am grateful to God for prompting me to go to the hospital at the last minute instead of trying to sleep off the cramping on my own at home.

> My parents-in-law visited us, and later my mother and grandfather. This was a wonderful, life-altering day! Thank you, God! This feels like a dream. Do we really have two beautiful boys? Are these really our children?

> Zed and Jay's temperatures dropped overnight, so they were put on warming mattresses. God, please help them to regulate their temperature.

Ash and I prayed for our boys each time we were near them. Our concerns about the possible developmental issues would not get our attention. We chose to fix our eyes on God and to look to Him for help.

I read this psalm to our boys:

I lift my eyes to the mountains where does my help come from? My help comes from the Lord, the maker of heaven and earth. He will not let your foot slip. He who watches over you will not slumber indeed he who watched over Israel will neither slumber nor sleep. The Lord watches over you. The Lord is at your right hand. The sun will not harm you by day, nor the moon by night. The Lord will keep you from all harm. He will watch over your life. The Lord will watch over your coming and your going both now and forever more. (Psalm 121:1–8 NIV)

As I prayed this morning, God showed me an image of angels' wings on either side of the cots that the boys are in. The wings were shielding the boys on both sides. The feathers were large and white. I looked again, and there was an angel standing at the foot of Zed's cot. The angel was very tall, but his head did not quite reach the roof of the hospital room. I looked to the left and saw that there was another angel standing at the foot of Jay's cot. The angel's feathers covered the sides of Jay's cot.

Thank you, God, for having sent angels to watch over each of our sons.

We hold on to hope for an excellent report of health for Zed and Jay and that they will continue to develop and grow well, even to the point of amazing others! The midwife who delivered our triplets three years ago visited me briefly. She was visibly moved as she expressed her joy at witnessing our happy ending.

Thursday, 26 October 2017

<u>Diary Entry</u>

> The doctors were happy with my body's healing after giving birth to the boys, so I was discharged from hospital on Wednesday. Ash and I were able to attend my best friend's wedding ceremony on Thursday afternoon.

Expressing milk into a machine while driving in the car from the wedding ceremony to the hospital was not how I imagined my first few days of motherhood would play out. Ash drove as carefully as he could to the hospital. The breast pump whirred effectively as I rehearsed the speech in my mind.

We thoroughly enjoyed our time with the boys and headed back to the reception while they napped. I candidly shared the speech with my best friend, her new husband, and their family and friends at the wedding reception. It was a wonderful occasion, during which we were all able to celebrate God's faithfulness in our lives. The moment I stepped up to give my speech, I was reminded of the picture God had shown me years ago of this very scene. The pregnant belly I had seen in that vision was actually my post-twin birth belly! I was astonished that even the wedding table was in the exact location as it had been in my vision. God is faithful!

Saturday, 28 October 2017

<u>Diary Entry</u>

> We were told this morning that Zed and Jay were doing so well that they were being moved to another hospital in our region.

I stood outside of the new hospital, overcome with emotion and moved to tears, as we watched Zed and Jay's cots being wheeled into their new ward. When we arrived in the Special Care Unit, the midwife reassured me that everything went well and that the boys were fine. Seeing them in their cots sent another flood of tears, and I could not hold back. The realization that I was already very much in love with our boys hit me unexpectedly. The staff and other patients could not have been kinder, and I found my place of peace being near our beautiful baby boys.

Wednesday, 1 November

<u>Diary Entry</u>

The boys had their first bath today.

Holding Zed's tiny body over the bath was the most tense but exhilarating experience. The nurse instructed me, and I tried my best to carefully follow each step. Babies—newborns in particular—certainly have a distinct smell. As I carefully held my firstborn twin over the sink of the bath, a rush of anxiety washed over me. Every muscle in my body tensed as I concentrated on holding on to this treasured child. His soft, delicate skin against my hand, I thanked God for how perfectly formed this little boy was. As I lowered Zed into the bath, I tried not to disturb the clip on his belly button and tried to move slowly so as not to make a mistake. The pressure to keep him safe overwhelmed me. The intensity was similar to what I imagined a surgeon faced when conducting a life-threatening surgery on a patient.

Even though my son cried as the water touched his unspoiled skin, I reassured him and vowed to myself that I would not allow anything to hurt him. As the warm water gently ran over his body, he began to settle, and his cry became a quiet whimper. Cautiously folding the soft towel around his body, I looked into my son's face and realized that he looked healthy and whole. Better than that, he was perfect!

Jay appeared to enjoy the water a little more, and I was surprised that he did not make a sound throughout the whole process. He appeared wonderfully content throughout the entire bathing routine. He sneezed briefly but continued relaxing in the warmness of the soothing water, completely unperturbed. A thought struck me that perhaps he would be like his mother, who thoroughly enjoyed swimming, baths, and any activity to do with water. Practice does make perfect, and I noticed that the second time round came more naturally; I was able to relax more during my second attempt at bathing a newborn. Examining Jay's face and body as I later dressed him, I observed that he was well formed, flawless, and complete. Testing results would prove later that there was no obvious genetic defect in either of our boys.

After bathing and resettling both boys in their cots, Ash, Zed, Jay, and I spent a few hours enjoying our time together as a family.

Breastfeeding was a new and difficult task at the beginning. As I grew in confidence, this undertaking brought me a deep sense of connection with our boys. I was filled with gratitude.

Friday, 3 November 2017

Diary Entry

> The boys are progressing well. Thank you, God. Ash and I gave them a bath on Wednesday, with a midwife's help, and they seemed to relax with the water. 'Kangacare' is

awesome and one of my favourite experiences. Holding both boys on my chest is comforting and helps me to bond with our twins.

Sunday, 12 November 2017

<u>Diary Entry</u>

Ash got up early on the Sunday to get the car seats ready. Our boys' temperatures and weights were progressing so well that they decided to allow us to go home. Each of the midwives and doctors marvelled at how quickly the boys had improved. This is a definite answer to prayer!

We packed up the clothing and the other baby gear, and then Ash and I placed our baby boys into their capsules for the first time. Zed and Jay slept as Ash made a few trips back to our car with our luggage. I sat on the feeding chair in the room, and I watched as the boys slept peacefully. Their beautiful faces were relaxed, content, and perfect. Their little bodies were tucked safely in the capsule, with cosy blankets covering them like soft cotton clouds. Their tiny heads were concealed under beautiful knitted woollen caps. This reminded me of their triplet brothers, whose heads were so much smaller. I still remembered the moment I saw a photo of Summer, Snow, and Sky's tiny heads covered with miniature versions of the knitted woollen caps. Tears sprang up into my eyes as I recalled our petite triplet boys resting in peace forever.

Zed's eyelids flickered for a moment, which broke me out of my mournful gaze. Jay's cheeks looked so smooth and flawless. Both boys breathed softly, almost undetectably, as it was nearly impossible to see the rising and lowering of their chests.

My heart ached as it grew with love for Zed and Jay.

Before our twins were born, I found it hard to believe that this would even be possible. My faith was small, but looking back now, I see that that faith was enough. We did not give up. We hoped against all odds, and here was our reward. Memories flashed through my mind of the years of anguish, the many failed pregnancy tests, the prayers said in tears, anger, or hope, and the words spoken by a living God who always knew that this day would come.

Overwhelmed with emotion, I struggled to control my tears. These were happy tears, grateful tears, and I gave myself permission to let them flow. God had taken our sadness and turned it into joy— or, as the psalm says, 'Weeping may stay for the night but rejoicing will come in the morning' (Psalm 30:5 NIV).

Ash and I endured a long night of pain and suffering as we struggled to become pregnant and subsequently faced the devastating loss of our triplet boys. We experienced the deepest form of grief that we had ever encountered as a couple. The desolation of our loss covered everything in our lives. I had almost given up completely. If it were not for my relationship with God and the love, faith, and hope that this connection brought, I might have given up altogether. However, God provided a new dawn. I was able to clutch on to the hope that only God could deliver.

Summer, Snow, and Sky reminded me to appreciate every minute of every day. Their lives taught me to be grateful for every breath and every heartbeat, because it was a gift from God. Our triplet boys' short but significant lives confirmed my belief that life begins at conception and continues until after we breathe our last breath. As a mother of five beautiful boys, I believe that one day in the future we will all be reunited in heaven for eternity.

In the meantime, Ash and I have been entrusted to look after Zed and Jay, our precious gifts from God. I could never forget that our twin boys were the answers to many prayers said by us and by our loved ones on our behalf. As a parent, I have realized that my children, each in his own unique way, have expanded my heart to make me a more compassionate person.

God fulfilled His promise to settle me as a happy mother, despite my struggles with fertility. My heart will always be filled with gratitude when I look into the eyes of my beautiful children Zed and Jay. They will remind me that God is good! Their lives will be a testimony of His kindness to me. I will share my story of God's amazing love with anyone who will listen.

'The Lord has done great things for us; and we are glad' (Psalm 126:3 ESV).

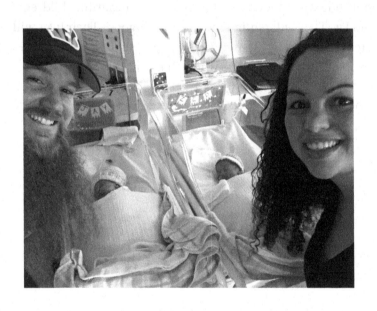

Scripture References

- New International Version Study Bible
- The Message Bible
- Christian Standard Bible
- New Living Translation
- English Standard Version

Book References

- *Good Grief*, by Granger Westberg

Music References

- 'You Are free', from the album *Photo Album* by Digital Prophets (2003)
- 'Calling' lyrics, by L. A. Field (2014)
- 'Oceans', by Hillsong United (2013)
- 'Princess', by L. A. Field (2016)

Printed in the United States
by Baker & Taylor Publisher Services